THE LECHEROUS UNIVERSITY

What Every Student and Parent Should Know About the Sexual Harassment Epidemic on Campus

Booklocker.com, Inc.
2002

THE LECHEROUS UNIVERSITY

What Every Student and Parent Should Know About the Sexual Harassment Epidemic on Campus

> **lecherous** (lĕch′ ər-əs); adjective; characterized by an excessive, uncontrollable, lustful appetite for sexual activity.

by

Charles J. Hobson, Ph.D.

and

Colleen L. Hobson, M.S., R.N.

with

Natalie Hobson, Research Assistant

Table of Contents

Dedication 1

Acknowledgements 3

Preface..5

CHAPTER 1 The Epidemic Incidence and Devastating Impact of Academic Sexual Harassment 7

CHAPTER 2 Knowing the Enemy—Profiling Rogue Faculty Sexual Predators and Their Techniques 21

CHAPTER 3 What is Academic Sexual Harassment? — Know Your Legal Rights! 33

CHAPTER 4 The Lecherous University in Operation— Women Beware!...53

CHAPTER 5 How Lecherous is Your University 63

CHAPTER 6 Preparing Yourself to be "Harassment-Proof" 81

CHAPTER 7 Filing a Complaint...91

CHAPTER 8 Collecting Evidence to Prove Your Case 115

CHAPTER 9 Surviving and Coping with an Experience of Academic Sexual Harassment 125

CHAPTER 10 Fighting Back—Specific Strategies to Combat Sexual Harassment on Campus 135

Appendix A Selected References and Resources..............................145

Appendix B University Sexual Harassment Prevention Rating Scale151

Appendix C U.S. Department of Education Office for Civil Rights
DISCRIMINATION COMPLAINT FORM 163
About the Authors 171

Dedication

This book is dedicated to the millions of women who have been sexually harassed by professors at U.S. colleges and universities. We hope you get the help you need to recover fully from your horrible experiences. Please join with us in fighting to end this scourge in higher education. One more victim is one too many.

We will donate 10% of the profit from sales of our book to the American Association of University Women's (AAUW) Legal Action Fund. This nonprofit organization provides financial assistance, attorney referrals, and a support system for female students interested in pursuing legal action for sex discrimination in higher education.

We will also donate 10% of the book profits to the Nazareth Home for medically challenged infants in East Chicago, Indiana.

Acknowledgements

Many individuals made invaluable, <u>positive</u> contributions to our efforts in writing this book. We would like to recognize and acknowledge their impact.

Sister Fidelis and Sister Barbara for their inspiration, prayers, support, and friendship.

Ruth Needleman for her unwavering support, inspiration, and courageous role model.

Anna Rominger for her moral support, encouragement, and sage legal insights.

Bala Arshanapalli for his empathy, active support, and enthusiastic encouragement.

Dawn Kesic for her understanding, empathy, and active support.

Dan Lowery for his moral and intellectual support, empathy, and inspiration.

Kathryn Heller for her empathy, moral support, and encouragement.

Marilyn Vasquez for her understanding, empathy, support, and advice.

Peter Kesheimer for his unwavering support and active encouragement.

Bob Moon for his active support and courageous role model in fighting campus sexual harassment.

Clara Connell for her empathy and unwavering support.

Jennifer Guziewicz for her empathy and active support.

Len Sporman for his understanding, empathy, and active support.

Other academic and professional colleagues to whom we are deeply indebted for their support and encouragement include: Don Coffin, Gary Lynch, Bill Nelson, Bert Scott, Dave Strupeck, Shyam Bhatia, Kathryn Lantz, Helen Harmon, Desila Rosetti, George Miga, George Wilkes, Marianne Milich, Linda Rooda, Bob Lovely, Marlene Ledbetter, Linda Delunas, Margaret Skurka, Bob Moran, Mark Sheldon, Judy Knapp, Thandubantu Iverson, Cathy Iovanella, Audrea Davis, Florence Sawicki, Sandy Mendoza, Cathy Tallos, Arlene Patterson, Nicki Lott, Cookie Van Scoyke, Karen Peterson, Deena Nardi, Attorneys Don Levinson and Monica McFadden, Judge John Pera, Dave Starkey, Bob Ward, and John Davies.

Liz Romeo for her tremendous efforts in preparing and formatting our book. Amy Crowder for her research and clerical support. Josh Hobson for his research and internet assistance.

On a _negative_ note, the resolve to write this book was also fueled by the many despicable faculty harassers we have had the misfortune of knowing and the spineless academic administrators who have allowed harassment to flourish on college campuses. Together, their brazen disregard for student civil rights and welfare has served as a powerful motivator to complete the book and start a national campaign to rid universities of faculty sexual predators and colluding administrators.

Inspiration for our title came from Billie Wright Dziech and Linda Weiner. They wrote a groundbreaking book in 1984 entitled, The Lecherous Professor— Sexual Harassment on Campus, later revised in 1990. They were among the first scholars to call attention to the harassment problem and focus blame on the intentional acts of unscrupulous faculty members. We are all indebted to the pioneering work of these two outstanding researchers.

Preface

Our book was written with one primary objective in mind—insuring that you and other college students are never victimized by faculty sexual harassment/sexual misconduct. According to a recently released report by the American Association of University Women (2000), over 75% of female college students are victimized by sexual harassment on campus and suffer a wide range of serious consequences.

We want to stop this appalling problem and firmly believe that one more victim is one too many. We hope to accomplish this by informing and empowering college students and their parents.

You've heard the old saying, "Knowledge is power." This is certainly true when it comes to preventing sexual harassment. By increasing your knowledge of the problem and how to prevent it, you will be in a much stronger position to aggressively protect your civil and consumer rights! Our goal is for you to become virtually "<u>harassment-proof</u>"!

Other faculty have criticized our book and approach to preventing campus sexual harassment as being "too one-sided" and "pro-student". We make no apologies for our intentionally and aggressively pro-student bias. We want to "level the playing field" and empower students to effectively defend their civil and consumer rights.

Given that the overwhelming majority of college students victimized by sexual harassment are women, and the majority of faculty harassers are men, our book focuses exclusively on those cases involving female students harassed by male professors. Our intent is not to suggest that male students are immune from sexual harassment or that female professors never harass students. Instead, we chose to concentrate the full attention of our book on what we perceive to be as the most prevalent and devastating manifestation of harassment on campus. Nevertheless, all of the advice we provide for female students is equally applicable to male students, and our goal is to stop the victimization of students, regardless of their gender.

All of the examples of sexual harassment in our book are real. We have set them apart from the rest of the text with italicized print. The examples are from two sources: (1) our direct personal experience with victims, witnesses, harassers, university administrators, faculty disciplinary files, and court materials, and (2) published accounts of sexual harassment on college campuses, in which case we provide a bibliographic citation.

In an effort to protect professors and further undermine student civil rights, many universities make an artificial distinction between faculty <u>sexual harassment</u> (which is illegal) and <u>sexual misconduct</u> (which is only professionally inappropriate). The distinction hinges on the apparent willingness of the female student to participate in sexual activities with the professor. Using this logic, unlawful sexual harassment only occurs when the student is clearly an unwilling participant; otherwise, the faculty member is simply guilty of unprofessional behavior—sexual misconduct.

We completely reject this disingenuous distinction! Given the overwhelming power advantage that professors have over students, willingness to participate is always suspect and should not serve as an excuse or license for sexual harassment. From our perspective, faculty sexual harassment and sexual misconduct are synonymous and both unlawful.

However, given that many universities continue to make the distinction, it is important to specify both offenses when requesting information about incidence statistics or faculty disciplinary records. Otherwise, schools can seriously underreport campus sexual harassment problems by simply reclassifying the cases as sexual misconduct. Thus, throughout the book, we use the phrasing "sexual harassment/sexual misconduct" to insure that underreporting does not occur.

In conclusion, we hope our book helps you and other college students avoid being victimized by faculty sexual predators. If you have been victimized, we hope our book can facilitate and guide your recovery. If we can help in any way, please contact us (chobson@iun.edu). Good luck.

Charlie and Colleen Hobson

CHAPTER 1

The Epidemic Incidence and

Devastating Impact of Academic Sexual Harassment

Kara had always wanted to be a pediatrician. She was a straight-A student throughout her undergrad curriculum and applied to several medical schools. She was accepted by her first choice and enrolled in the Fall.

The professor in one of her four classes asked her to come by his office for a brief meeting. Of course she agreed. Upon arriving at the office, the professor invited her to have a seat and then closed the door. In a very direct, matter-of-fact manner, he informed Kara that providing sexual favors to him was an informal part of the orientation program for incoming female students, and wanted to schedule a rendezvous at a nearby motel.

Kara at first thought he was joking, but then quickly realized he was not. She was stunned and outraged, and categorically refused to cooperate. The professor then threatened her with a failing grade if she did not comply, regardless of how well she did in the course. He also informed her that an "F" would result in probation for the following semester. Finally, he warned her against filing a complaint, asserting that his word as a distinguished med school professor carried more weight than hers and that he and his faculty colleagues would insure that she failed academically.

Kara pleaded with him to stop the harassment and treat her as any other student. The professor refused.

Although she studied hard and knew the material well, Kara received an "F" on her midterm. She appealed to the professor to evaluate her test objectively and change her grade. He was unyielding and reiterated that the only way to pass the course was to have sex with him.

Tragically, the harassing professor gave Kara an "F" for the class and she was placed on probation. When enrolling for spring semester classes, she discovered that the same professor taught another core class that she was required to take.

Before the semester began, Kara went to his office and once again pleaded for fairness and objectivity. The professor responded by informing her that a second "F" in one of her courses would result in expulsion. She still refused to submit and hoped that he would somehow change his mind.

When Kara received her midterm test grade in that class of "F", she decided to immediately withdraw from the course and drop out of school altogether. During her 7-month ordeal, Kara had lost 30 pounds, developed a bleeding ulcer, and been diagnosed and treated as clinically depressed. At one point, she seriously considered suicide as a way to end her hellish experience. Ultimately, she gave up her lifelong dream of being a pediatrician and never returned to med school.

Kara's case and others like it occur far more often in academia than most people are aware. The purpose of this chapter is to present information about the widespread incidence of academic sexual harassment and the devastating consequences experienced by most victims. Our hope is that you and other readers will better understand the magnitude and severity of this horrible problem and mobilize efforts to prevent it.

Epidemic Rates of Victimization

In a book entitled, A License for Bias–Sex Discrimination, Schools and Title IX, the widely respected American Association of University Women (AAUW) concluded that more than 75% of women in colleges and universities have been affected by sexual harassment. This translates into a staggering number of over 5 million victims!

Two quotes attributable to female students in Billie Wright Dziech's and Linda Weiner's book, The Lecherous Professor, provide compelling evidence of this widespread problem.

> *"Any woman who goes in for higher education, unless she goes to Bob Jones University, is bound to tangle sexually with a professor."*
> *"I've had several experiences with profs staring at me, bumping into me, making suggestive remarks. They're silly and boring, but they also*

repulse me. When I talk to my friends, they're not surprised; they just say that it happens all the time."

Studies at specific schools indicate just how blatant and common the harassment is. At one institution, 9% of all graduate women reported receiving direct sexual propositions from male professors. At another school, 5% of all female students reported harassment involving sexual bribery–grades for sex. Finally, an anonymous survey of 235 male professors at a large research university revealed that 26% admitted to having had sex with students!

The problem of sexual harassment in higher education has truly reached epidemic proportions. If we consider those women who have been directly victimized over the last 20 years, as well as their concerned parents, the total easily exceeds 50 million.

Are you shocked by any of these statistics? Most people are. Universities have done a tremendous job in hiding this disgraceful problem from public view.

Since schools are not required by law to publish sexual harassment incidence rates, with few exceptions, they do not. Thus, virtually no one, including current/prospective students and their parents, has any clear idea of the grave risks that coeds today face on college campuses.

As a female student, if you knew that you faced a 75% chance of being sexually harassed at school, how would you respond? Would this be okay with you? If your parents knew that you faced this substantial threat, how would they respond? Would this be okay with them?

Universities are afraid of what these answers might be and how students and parents might react to the epidemic of campus sexual harassment. Consequently, schools go to great lengths to conceal this information from the public. Chapter 4 provides an in-depth look at how universities operate and fail to protect student civil and consumer rights.

High-Risk, Harasser Target Groups. Research has shown that faculty sexual predators exhibit a tendency to concentrate more of their attention on women in certain target groups, principally as a function of their increased vulnerability. Incidence rates tend to be higher for female graduate students, women of color, and women with disabilities.

Many explanations have been offered for this reprehensible targeting strategy, all of which involve heightened vulnerability. Graduate students often receive some form of substantial financial assistance from their university—a teaching/research assistantship, fellowship, and/or scholarship. This support is often contingent upon the recommendations of the student's faculty advisor—presenting an opportunity for sexual bribery (sex in exchange for continued financial support).

Faculty advisors also exercise near complete and total control over key stages in a student's academic progress. Advisors make subjective, essentially unchallengeable, decisions to: (a) pass or fail a student in a required class, (b) pass or fail a student who has taken a comprehensive or preliminary exam over a field of expertise, (c) pass or fail a student's oral thesis or dissertation defense, and (d) accept or reject a student's final written thesis or dissertation. These are all monumental decisions in a student's life—once again, providing ample opportunities for sexual bribery.

An anecdote cited in Bernice Sandler's and Robert Shoop's <u>Sexual Harassment on Campus</u> illustrates the plight many female graduate students face.

> *"[My faculty advisor] cried and so forth [about his marital problems] and I responded as if he were my friend. It was the wrong thing to do; he was soon making real [sexual] advances. I was utterly repulsed but I was terrified to say no. He just had too much authority over me. It was absolute. It was even more than the authority that a boss has over you in a job; it has parental aspects to it because this whole graduate experience is an apprenticeship system . . . It always seemed at the time that I would rather be sexually exploited than risk my whole career. You see, nobody else [other than your major advisor] really knows that much about what you're doing academically. The whole way they judge you is by what your advisor says to them at coffee and over lunch and so forth. Everything depends on his opinion and I thought if I get him pissed off at a personal level he's going to communicate negatively about me to the others. I knew I couldn't overcome that because I'd seen it happen before, and once you get a reputation for not being a good student they don't ever give you a chance to perform otherwise."*

In another instance, a young woman was nearing completion of her doctorate in psychology, after five long years of study. Her major professor and dissertation advisor invited her for a collegial dinner at his apartment, ostensibly to celebrate her soon to be completed Ph.D. After dinner, he began to make sexual advances, which were initially rebuffed by the young woman. As his frustration mounted, he aggressively told her that his final signature on her dissertation was contingent on her sexual cooperation. He then proceeded to forcibly rape her and threatened dire consequences if she filed a complaint. Tragically, the devastated woman suffered severe emotional trauma from this event, spent many tortured years in therapy, never fully recovered, and never reported it.

Women of color are also frequently targeted by faculty sexual predators for many of the following reasons: (a) an increased likelihood that the student is receiving some form of financial aid, which the harasser can threaten to terminate, (b) a higher probability that the young woman is a first-generation college student, possessing little familiarity, understanding, or experience with higher education and what to expect, (c) foreign-exchange students who must maintain an appropriate visa in order to remain in the United States provide harassers with the opportunity to threaten deportation, and (d) a strong, culturally-based deference to authority, men, older persons, and/or educators.

In one particularly unfortunate case, a distraught Oriental-American student consulted with her family after having been sexually propositioned by her male professor. He had promised an "A" in exchange for a night at a local motel. As recent arrivals to the United States, no one in her family was familiar with the functioning of higher education. Thus, based upon their own cultural traditions, her parents reluctantly advised her not to "make waves" or upset the professor and possibly jeopardize her academic career. The young woman followed their advice and submitted to the harasser's sexual advances.

Thompson Publishing Group's Educator's Guide to Controlling Sexual Harassment (March, 1999) reported a recent legal case involving a graduate exchange student and a professor who helped foreign students with their immigration and visa forms. According to the young woman's court testimony, the professor forced her to have sex with him repeatedly or he would have her deported. Additional allegations included verbal and physical abuse. Although the student contended that she tried to end the relationship, the professor insisted that she had no choice if she wished to remain in the United States.

Finally, faculty sexual predators frequently target women with disabilities. Their perceived vulnerability is heightened by the following factors: (a) an increased likelihood of receiving financial aid from the university, which the harasser could threaten to terminate, (b) lower levels of self-esteem and self-confidence, related to their disability, and (c) potentially increased susceptibility to flattery and attention from a harasser.

Devastating Impact of Sexual Harassment

Billie Wright Dziech and Linda Weiner, in their book, The Lecherous Professor, provide a stunning anecdote of the damage done to young women by faculty sexual predators.

> *"Perhaps this is shocking, but an accepted norm in our institution was faculty-student affairs. Ours was a small campus in a somewhat isolated town, and very bright young female students were forced to spend considerable time with the extremely intelligent, predominantly male faculty. When affairs inevitably resulted, there often appeared to be an element of glamour in them for some of the women. Frequently, these were their first sexual experiences. I suspect that their previous encounters with men their own age had been problematic, and the faculty reinforced their sense of alienation from their peers. The women were told that they were too bright, that they would be too threatening to men their own age. In some ways, that was true, so they often responded to sexual attention from younger male faculty by supposing that intellectual equality implied the male could be trusted to guide them into other areas of life.*

> *However intelligent they were, the students were actually at an emotional disadvantage. In fact, most of the affairs were sad to watch because the women didn't really know what was happening. The relationships were usually fairly visible, since there wasn't any real disapproval. They might last two or three months, and the student would appear to feel totally in control of the situation, almost proud of it. It wasn't unusual to see the faculty member right in the dorm, using the floor john.*

> *Then when the affair broke up, the student would often be a basket case. She would have to watch the next affair, see her ex-lover go on to another student, possibly even in the same dormitory.*

In the four years I was there, I remember only one case of "true love", of a faculty-student relationship that lasted with any integrity. It was an older female in her mid-twenties and a new faculty member who was single and just a few years older. All the others were just casual affairs for the men, and the women who became involved with them never realized that until it was too late.

Academic sexual harassment has a devastating impact on victims! Experiences like the one suffered by Kara in the beginning of the chapter and the young women in the above example are all too common. Consequences of being victimized have been documented in the following major categories: (a) psychological, (b) physical/medical, and (c) behavioral/academic.

Psychological. The most common psychological symptoms include:

- increased stress and anxiety
- heightened risk of depression
- lower self-esteem
- intense feelings of guilt and shame
- decreased motivation and initiative
- fear of sexual intimacy
- suicidal thoughts and intentions

Physical/Medical. Sexual harassment victims suffer a number of very serious physical/medical conditions, including:

- ulcers and other digestive disorders
- high blood pressure
- sleep disorders
- eating disorders
- significant fluctuations in body weight
- impaired immune system functioning
- increased frequency and duration of illness
- sexual dysfunction
- increased risk of suicide attempts

Behavioral/Academic. Harassment victims typically experience one or more of the following behavioral/academic outcomes:

- increased classroom tardiness and absenteeism
- decreased classroom performance and lower grades
- higher likelihood of withdrawing from classes
- forced changing of majors and/or institutions
- greater probability of quitting higher education altogether

Taken together, the above consequences pose an overwhelming threat to the health and well being of any young woman.

Sadly, these consequences can be even more destructive to women in two special subgroups. First, students with serious, psychological/medical problems are particularly vulnerable. The cumulative impact of the harassment experience and their pre-existing condition can absolutely shatter their lives.

A second high-risk subgroup consists of women with a history of sexual abuse. For these student victims, in addition to the immediate damage from the harassment experience, they are also likely to relive the trauma of the earlier abuse. This significantly intensifies their suffering.

The Toll on Parents as Victims

When Diane answered the phone that evening, she immediately knew something was definitely wrong by the tone in her daughter Carla's voice. She was right. One of Carla's professors had attempted to sexually assault her at his home earlier that afternoon. She was sobbing uncontrollably on the phone.

After unsuccessfully trying to calm her down, Diane insisted that she and Carla's father, Tom, drive down to school and bring her home. The offer seemed to bring immediate relief and comfort to Carla.

The 3-1/2 hour drive seemed to take forever. Diane and Tom had worried about what might happen to their daughter while she was away at school, but they never dreamed that a professor would try to sexually attack her. Both were concerned about how this incident would affect her psychologically and academically.

They were outraged that something like this could be allowed to happen on a college campus. Tom especially was consumed with a seething rage. He was threatening to go directly to the professor's house and beat him senseless. Diane immediately cautioned against the use of violence and recommended filing a complaint with the university. She was confident that the institution would severely punish the professor and probably fire him.

Diane's soothing words helped Tom to finally calm down. They both agreed that their first priority should be helping Carla cope with this traumatic experience. Tom suggested that she see a therapist he knew at the local community mental health center and Diane agreed wholeheartedly. They committed to work together as a family to help their daughter through the crisis.

When Tom and Diane picked up Carla late that evening, her eyes were red and swollen and she was still sobbing—but obviously relieved and happy to see her parents. During the drive home, she related what the professor had done to her.

She had been invited to his home to discuss an important research project and her possible role as a student assistant. After briefly talking about the project, the professor began to make comments about how sexy and beautiful she was. Carla became very tense and apprehensive about what might happen next.

The professor offered her a drink and walked toward his bar. When he passed behind Carla's chair, he stopped and fondled her breast. As she jumped up, he tried to kiss her.

Carla ran for the front door. The professor tried to block her exit and grabbed her arm. She pulled away and quickly opened the door and left.

Carla ran all the way back to her dorm room where she locked herself in. She was terrified and angry, and unable to stop crying for over an hour.

Tom and Diane were heartbroken to hear what had happened to Carla. They tried to comfort her and talked about the idea of seeing a therapist. Tom's rage and desire for revenge surged again, but he kept his feelings to himself and tried to maintain the focus on helping Carla.

After a restful week at home and two visits with the therapist, Carla felt strong enough to return to school. She dropped the class with the harassing professor and went to the Student Affairs Office to file a complaint. Carla was *interviewed by an assistant affirmative action officer and also submitted a written statement of what happened.*

The university official promised an investigation of the complaint. A letter would be sent to Carla once the process was completed.

Carla and her parents waited over four months for this letter to come. In essence, the university concluded that there was insufficient evidence that a violation had occurred. The professor had vehemently denied the allegations. He contended that, since he was foreign-born, Carla had perhaps misinterpreted his friendly behaviors. Under any circumstances, the case was closed as far as the university was concerned.

Carla and her parents were stunned at the news. They felt betrayed by the university and disgusted that the professor was not disciplined. Tom insisted that justice had not been served by the university's investigation and convinced Diane and Carla to initiate a lawsuit against the university and professor.

During the discovery process, they learned that there were six similar complaints against the same professor within the previous five years. With a renewed sense of optimism and vindication, they were increasingly confident about their chances in court.

In preparing its defense, the university scheduled a deposition for Carla, to question her about what happened. Given her age of 19, the university attorney agreed to allow Tom and Diane to sit in the room during the deposition, as long as they promised to remain silent.

After obtaining general information about her background, the university attorney began a line of vicious questioning meant to intimidate both Carla and her parents. First, the attorney maintained that Carla was doing poorly in the professor's class. This was absolutely false, but the attorney continued to insist that she was a poor student.

Diane was outraged and Tom was about ready to explode. He did when the next question was asked. "Didn't you go to the professor's house with the intent of seducing him to get a better grade?"

Carla was shocked by the question and began crying uncontrollably. Tom exploded and began cursing at the university's lawyer. Carla's attorney quickly intervened and led Tom out of the room.

After composing herself, Carla answered the question with an emphatic "no." Next, the attorney asked, "Wasn't your attempted seduction of the professor consistent with your slut-like behavior throughout high school?"

Diane burst out saying, "How dare you insult my daughter that way!" Carla's attorney was once again forced to intervene and escort Diane out of the room. When Tom saw her and heard what had happened, he demanded that the proceedings stop. Diane quickly agreed.

They would not allow this tortuous treatment of their daughter to continue. Tom and Diane went back into the deposition room, hugged Carla, and left together. They immediately dropped the lawsuit.

Carla dropped out of college and never returned. She and her parents saw a therapist for several months and then stopped going. All three of them continue to harbor intense feelings of anger, resentment, frustration, and betrayal.

While women exploited by sexual harassment suffer horribly, their parents also agonize over the experience. Learning that your daughter has been sexually victimized is one of a parent's worst nightmares.

It is absolutely heart wrenching to see the damage done to your "little girl", whom you have loved, nurtured, and supported all of her life. Intense feelings of outrage, betrayal of trust in the university, revenge, and frustration are paralyzing.

Your first instinct is to help and comfort your daughter. This is quickly followed by a near obsessive desire for justice and punishment.

At this point in the process, most parents are confronted with a jarring reality. Only 2-3% of women victimized by faculty sexual predators actually file a formal complaint. The overwhelming majority suffers in silence, with no hope for restitution or punishment for the offenders.

Although it may initially be difficult to understand why your daughter would not want to file a complaint, there are a host of powerful disincentives that discourage this behavior. First, and perhaps most importantly, filing a complaint forces your daughter to relive her painful experience over and over again. She will be asked to put her allegations in writing. She will be interviewed and re-interviewed. She will be asked to appear before a hearing committee and possibly an appeals committee. She may be asked to meet with the harasser to allow him an opportunity to hear her charges and respond. All of this is incredibly stressful and compels your daughter to repeatedly revisit the initial trauma.

Most victims simply want to put the harassing experience behind them and get on with their lives. After witnessing the anguish their daughter goes through in discussing the harassment, most parents end up supporting the decision not to file a complaint. They want to spare their daughter further suffering.

A second potent reason not to file a complaint is the overriding pro-faculty bias that pervades most college campuses. Universities are staunch defenders of faculty rights and privileges, even at the expense of student civil rights. Filing a complaint against a professor is an "uphill battle" at best, with the odds strongly against the student.

Third, there is always a potential risk of retaliation against a student who dares file a complaint against a professor. Given the subjectivity inherent in academic evaluations, the harasser and his supporters can retaliate with

- poor or failing grades
- revocation of financial support or work-study jobs
- negative recommendations for scholarships, academic awards, graduate school and employment, and
- rejection of thesis or dissertation projects

Finally, any woman who contemplates legal action against an institution and/or professor should be prepared for aggressive, vicious treatment by opposing attorneys. Their goal will be to intimidate the student and argue that she initiated the sexual activity because either (a) she is and has always been sexually promiscuous, or (b) she was trying to get a better grade in return for sex. The harasser will be portrayed as an unsuspecting victim. Such treatment by a university attorney is nearly unbearable for an already suffering student.

Given these powerful obstacles, it is easy to see why most sexual harassment victims do not file a formal complaint. It is also easy to see why most parents ultimately support this type of decision by their daughter. They simply do not want to see her suffer any more than she already has. Thus, while most student victims of sexual harassment suffer in silence, the same is also true for their parents.

For parents, seeing your daughter suffer and knowing that the harasser got away with it is a crushing burden to carry in life. To make matters even worse, you know that the faculty predator will harass again, harming someone else's daughter.

All of this poses a vexing dilemma for concerned parents. Your daughter's happiness and welfare are foremost priorities. You want the wounds to heal from her harassment experience and you never want her retraumatized again. At the same time, you know that if no one ever files a complaint against a harasser, he will never be brought to justice and will continue to victimize unsuspecting students in the future.

If your daughter's wounds are healed and she has regained her mental, emotional, and physical health, we encourage you to seriously consider filing a formal complaint against the university and professor. We discuss how to do this in Chapter 7. She will need your full support throughout the complaint process.

If successful, you and your daughter will achieve some sense of closure or resolution to her harassment experience. You will also strike a blow against faculty sexual predators and universities that encourage them.

Unfortunately, as mentioned at the beginning of this chapter, the AAUW's stunning conclusion that 3 out of 4 women in college are affected by sexual harassment means that the overwhelming odds are against your daughter. There is a 75% likelihood that she will be victimized. Hopefully, our book will help you beat these odds and prevent your daughter from being sexually harassed. If she is victimized, we hope our advice can help you deal more effectively with the daunting challenges that both you and your daughter will face.

Conclusions

Academic sexual harassment is clearly a widespread problem at U.S. universities that you and other female students are likely to be exposed to during your collegiate careers. As we discussed, the consequences of being victimized can be truly devastating. Thus, it is imperative that you understand fully what the problem involves, develop a solid personal plan to prevent this catastrophe from happening to you, and actively support efforts to prevent it from happening to others.

CHAPTER 2

Knowing the Enemy—Profiling Rogue Faculty Sexual

Predators and Their Techniques

"If you put me at a table with food [coeds], I eat." This was how a biology *professor described his insatiable appetite for sex with undergraduate students. He saw them as a "perk" of the job and looked forward to a "new crop" at the beginning of every semester.*

This disgusting attitude is more prevalent among male faculty members and negatively impacts more female students than most people would ever imagine. The purpose of this chapter is to help you better understand faculty harassers and the tactics they use on their target victims. By "knowing the enemy" and how they operate, we hope that you and others can avoid being victimized.

As you might suspect, the research on faculty harassers is somewhat limited. Who would volunteer to serve as a subject in a study on sexual predators? There is however a small body of research on harasser characteristics and techniques. In this chapter, we will combine these results and our personal experiences with hundreds of women victims and scores of faculty harassers at many different institutions.

Common Harasser Characteristics

Let's be perfectly clear about the faculty sexual predators we profile. These are individuals who knowingly, willingly, and enthusiastically engage repeatedly in unlawful activities by violating the civil rights of their victims, inflicting great harm in the process. They are the brethren of bin Laden in the academic world and terrorize the innocent, powerless, and vulnerable. While all of the characteristics that we will identify and discuss in this chapter do not apply to every harasser, together they provide a useful description of most faculty sexual predators.

Hostility Toward Women. Most faculty sexual predators harbor a deep-seated hostility toward women, often bordering on hatred or misogyny. This intense devaluing allows harassers to view the violation of victim civil rights as somehow acceptable, legitimate, and appropriate. In addition to harassing behaviors, there are typically a number of additional manifestations of this hostility.

For example, one serial harassing social science professor was well known for his outspoken attacks on anything related to women. This included the university's Women's Studies Department, affirmative action, equal employment opportunity, diversity initiatives, the National Organization for Women (NOW), and feminism. He routinely made insulting, embarrassing comments to both his female students and faculty colleagues.

History of Unsuccessful Relationships with Women. Given the extreme hostility toward women mentioned above, it is not surprising to find that most harassers are unable to have healthy, successful relationships with members of the opposite sex. This can be evidenced by a series of failed marriages, the complete absence of female friends or colleagues, and strained or nonexistent relations with female family members—mother, sister, aunt, etc.

One 45-year-old psychology professor was in the process of finalizing his sixth divorce in 15 years. In each instance, he had married a favored graduate student, enamored with his academic power and prestige. These relationships quickly disintegrated and resulted in acrimonious divorces.

Physically Unattractive/Sexually Undesirable. One consistent observation that we have made throughout our experience with victims and harassers is that faculty sexual predators can generally be characterized as physically unattractive and sexually undesirable. Members of the university community often view their appearance and demeanor as repulsive. This obvious shortcoming serves as a powerful motivator to faculty predators in seeking forced sex from student victims, over whom they wield considerable power.

Immoral and Dishonest. Faculty sexual predators typically have weak or nonexistent moral standards that allow them to rationalize their abuse of female students. They all demonstrate a capacity to deceive and lie easily. This serves them well in any complaint investigation when they can calmly and convincingly blame the entire episode on the "scheming" student and dramatically portray themselves as the real victim.

The disgusting ability to lie easily and well was frequently demonstrated by former President Clinton during the Monica Lewinsky scandal. His disgraceful, "slick" propensity to deceive and conceal information about his abusive relationship with the young White House intern prompted a Democratic senator to conclude that Clinton was not just a good liar, "he was a <u>damned</u> good liar!"

<u>High Comfort Level with Dominator Role</u>. The twisted personalities and moral standards that characterize most faculty harassers allow them to feel comfortable in their roles as dominators over helpless victims. These ruthless predators eagerly relish and abuse the power imbalance, finding pleasure in harassing, humiliating, and tormenting female students.

<u>Clear Grasp of Gatekeeper Function</u>. Faculty sexual predators clearly understand the critically important roles that they play in facilitating or blocking student academic progress. They emphasize and accentuate their control over students and abuse this power by forcing sexual compliance.

<u>Knowledge of University Functioning</u>. Most harassers have an acute understanding of how universities function and the deference given to professors. They truly know how the system works and they use it to their advantage to victimize students. These predators know exactly what your civil rights are, but they have found a multitude of ways to violate them with little likelihood of discovery or punishment. You should never underestimate how cunning and manipulative faculty harassers can be in utilizing the university environment to exploit students.

For example, a life sciences professor created a hostile, intimidating learning environment in his classroom for decades through the use of unconscionable, offensive slides, (one photograph of a pop bottle inserted into a female orifice), displays, and comments. He brazenly defended himself by asserting that university administrators had known about his conduct for years and not taken any action—thus implicitly endorsing or accepting his behaviors. He threatened to respond to any future disciplinary actions with a lawsuit against the institution. This depraved thug has intimidated a series of weak-willed administrators and he continues to violate student civil rights in his classroom.

Serial Violations. Most faculty sexual predators are serial harassers who violate student civil rights throughout their tenure as professors. Some research indicates that many harassers are engaged with multiple students simultaneously.

When unexpected complaints are filed against faculty predators, a common defense offered is that this is the first and only time in their careers that they have ever succumbed to temptation and harassed a student. A much more accurate description in most of these cases is that this is the first time they have been caught.

Furthermore, "getting caught" once will rarely convince a faculty predator to reform his behavior. There may be a temporary halt to harassing tactics until "the heat is off", but most predators quickly return to their old habits.

Social Radar. One very disgusting characteristic that many harassers share is an uncanny ability to identify target victims who appear to be passive, timid, deferential to authority, likely to submit to sexual advances, and unlikely to file a complaint. Faculty predators use a variety of nonverbal, verbal, and academic cues to quickly assess coed susceptibility.

For example, failure to make direct eye contact when a harasser is talking to you or you are responding sends a clear message that you are intimidated, not assertive, and likely to be "easy prey." When dealing with faculty predators, it is critical to carefully control your verbal and nonverbal behavior so as to send a powerful message that you will not tolerate or submit to their advances. This topic is covered in more detail in Chapter 6.

Final Note. The above characteristics combine to make the typical faculty sexual predator a formidable force and threat to unsuspecting coeds. Tragically, although psychological assessment tools are available to measure characteristics of sexual offenders, there is no university to our knowledge currently using them to screen new faculty hires. We strongly believe that the use of psychological screening methods could sharply reduce the number of harassers that are ultimately hired.

Common Harasser Techniques

Perhaps the best discussion of the most common techniques used by faculty sexual predators can be found in Dziech's and Weiner's groundbreaking book in 1984, The Lecherous Professor (a second edition was published in 1990). We will build on their work and that of other researchers, along with our own experiences, in describing how harassers typically operate.

While many harassers have a favored "M.O.", most are sufficiently cunning to change their tactics to best take advantage of their target victim. Familiarity with these approaches will hopefully allow you to quickly identify and resist them.

Gate-Keeper/Power-Broker. This is perhaps the most direct and blatant technique used by harassers. Professors who utilize this approach are acutely aware of their roles as decision makers, wielding significant power over the academic and employment futures of their students. For example, faculty commonly make decisions such as: (a) assigning a passing or failing grade in a required course; (b) approving or disapproving thesis and dissertation projects; (c) recommending students for desirable scholarships, internships, or special academic programs; (d) approving or disapproving students for graduation, certification, and/or licensure; and (e) recommending students for graduate school or employment. All of these kinds of decisions are critically important to the academic success of students.

Faculty sexual predators typically employ the gate-keeper/power-broker approach by blatantly propositioning a female student in private, offering a favorable decision in exchange for sexual favors. Their credo can be summed up by "an 'A' for a lay." The offer is typically coupled with a threatened negative decision if the student fails to cooperate. Finally, the predator warns of the dire consequences associated with attempting to file a complaint. He emphasizes his stature and credibility at the institution and asserts that "his word" would be believed over that of a disgruntled, academically challenged student intent on retaliation for a poor grade.

All of this can be quite shocking and intimidating to the target victim. Unfortunately, many young women feel powerless to resist this brazen abuse of professorial power and submit. An actual example will illustrate how ruthless faculty sexual predators can be in applying this technique.

A professor of education knew that many of his summer graduate students who were public school teachers needed to pass his class in order to retain state certification and thus keep their jobs in local schools. During the course of the summer semester, he carefully scrutinized his female students to identify those that he felt were attractive and unlikely to resist his advances or file a complaint.

At the end of the semester, he would automatically assign his target victims "Incompletes" or "I's" as final grades, regardless of how well they performed academically in class. He knew that an "I" would prevent recertification and thus jeopardize their employment status.

When shocked victims received their "I's" in the mail, most immediately telephoned his office to question their grades. He insisted that they schedule an appointment to discuss the matter.

When a student arrived at his office, he invited her in and promptly shut the door. At that point, he made his repugnant offer to remove the "I" if she agreed to join him at a local motel.

Another blatant example of this technique can be found in Billie Wright Dziech's and Linda Weiner's book, The Lecherous Professor.

> *"Well, my freshman year I took a class. I didn't understand all of the readings, and by the time the final came around, I found myself with an 'F.' So I asked him if I could talk to him about grades in his office. So I went to his office and he gave me a choice—either be with him or take the 'F.' I was attracted to him a little, but there was no way I could take the 'F.' So I met him at his house, and I spent three hours with him in his bed. I had to close my eyes and pretend that I was with my boyfriend. I felt dirty, but I didn't get the 'F.' He gave me a 'D.' Was it worth it? Yes and no. I felt it was something I had to do to save myself."*

Intellectual Seducer. Predators who prefer a more subtle yet equally devastating approach often begin by showering intellectual flattery on an unsuspecting woman, both publicly in class and in private. Their intent is to first intellectually seduce the young woman and then take advantage of her sexually.

The intense attention and recognition shown by a prominent faculty member can be overwhelming, ego enhancing, and very difficult to resist.

One foreign language professor was a habitual abuser of this technique. In every introductory class, he would attempt to identify an attractive first-year female student, who had exceptional language skills and was deemed too impressionable and passive to file a complaint. After frequent in-class flattery, this predator would ask his target victim to schedule an office visit in the near future.

When she arrived, he would laud her excellent grasp of the language and superb accent. He continued by expressing a sincere desire to recommend her for a highly prestigious overseas study program.

Of course, his victims were exhilarated with this attention and flattery from a "respected" professor. They enthusiastically agreed to be nominated.

The next step in the predator's plan was to emphasize that the letter of recommendation for the overseas program must be hand-delivered in a sealed envelop within the following two days. He "graciously" offered to find time in his busy schedule to prepare a letter by the next afternoon.

He then asked his target victim if she could come by his house the following afternoon to pick up and deliver the letter. Once again, he was met with an overwhelmingly positive response.

Upon arriving at his house, the young woman discovered the door slightly open with a note to come in and proceed up to the third floor. Several unsuspecting, trusting coeds, over a period of nearly 10 years, followed his instructions and were stunned when confronted by the nude predator offering an invitation to have sex and get to know each other better.

Counselor/Advisor. Another subtle yet powerful harassment approach involves the bastardization of the professor's legitimate role as a counselor or advisor. Faculty sexual predators exploit unsuspecting students who seek advice by taking advantage of their vulnerability. Often times, this begins by the predator displaying feelings of concern and empathy for a student, thus winning her confidence. Once achieved, sexual advances quickly follow.

A particularly reprehensible example will illustrate how this technique is employed. A psychology professor "specialized" in "counseling" coeds who were upset with boyfriend rejections. When he discovered that one of his students had experienced such a break-up, he would initially invite them to his office. The ostensible purpose was to help them deal with the emotional stress.

The professor masterfully played the role of a supportive, understanding, empathetic advisor. Follow-up help sessions were quickly scheduled for local restaurants or bars, and eventually the predator's apartment or home.

Throughout this process, the disguised harasser would continuously praise his target's qualities of beauty, personality, and sexuality, reinforcing her damaged ego. He would criticize her ex-boyfriend as a fool who did not know what a wonderful companion he had.

When the "moment was right", the predator would strike by initiating sexual advances. More often than not, the vulnerable, trusting, unsuspecting coeds would submit to his advances.

Confidant/Friend. Predators who use this approach attempt to befriend unsuspecting students by initially treating them as equals and sharing intimate personal information. This strategy is often implemented at off-campus locations like restaurants, bars, parties, or even the harasser's apartment/home. Once the predator has won the confidence and friendship of his victim, he moves quickly to exploit this trust with his sexual advances.

One sociology professor was notorious for hosting parties for undergraduate students at his home. Ample alcohol was readily available to all of the underaged students and heavy drinking was the norm. The predator would focus his attention on a target victim, engaging in intimate one-on-one conversation on the porch, while encouraging continued drinking. When the "time was right", the predator would invite his new friend to stay after the party was over. Once everyone else had departed, he would exploit this "friendship", initiating sexual advances. With few exceptions, his victims succumbed.

A second example of this approach can be found in Billie Wright Dziech's and Linda Weiner's book, The Lecherous Professor.

"[He's] like a rabid wolf hovering at the edge of a sheep pack—the incoming class of freshmen.

When he's selected a girl who's unusually attractive, intelligent, and naive, he moves right in. Believe me, he's predatory—I've seen him in action. First, he'll 'rap and relate' with the freshman over drinks at the college bar. In a couple of weeks, he has her dizzy with the 'existential nihilism of Sartre' or 'archetypal patterns of Jung.' All this may sound exciting, but the results are tragicomic. Two years ago, he 'shared' a girl with a friend of his, another faculty member. The three of them made it while watching a particularly beautiful sunrise—very aesthetic, you know. His current ploy is backgammon. You see him shaking those dice at a table in the rathskeller with this hazy-eyed kid. Several dormitory assistants have seen him leaving her room at six in the morning, and campus security once caught him with a student in the stacks of the library. You can guess what he found.

Is Tom exploiting his pupils? You bet he is. Does he know what he's doing? Of course. Is the administration aware of what he's up to? Sure they are, but these days, to get fired for what they used to call 'moral turpitude,' you'd have to rape an entire cheerleading squad at half time. Tom's like a pothead turned loose in a Twinkies factory."

Opportunist. Harassers using this technique engage in apparently harmless, yet sexually provocative and inappropriate touching of students, commenting about their appearance or personal lives, and sharing sexually explicit jokes and stories. Often disguised as humor, these tactics are intended to solicit expressions of interest on the part of students. The predator then takes advantage of these opportunities by pursuing interested coeds.

A history professor used this basic technique in all of his classes. It involved open flirting with students before and after class. While attempting to be humorous, he would comment on how attractive and sexy coeds appeared and asked questions about their social lives. One of his favorite lines was to assert that, if he were a college student, he would certainly want to date these coeds.

Inevitably, someone would engage the predator in this type of classroom banter. He would then capitalize on this "opportunity" by asking the coed to stay after class or visit his office. Sexual advances would soon follow.

A more subtle and cunning, yet equally devious, variation of the Opportunist technique can be seen in the following anecdote from M. Cynara

Stites' chapter in Michele Paludi's book, <u>Sexual Harassment on College Campuses</u>.

> *"Through the journal [required for the class], I began to share my personal experiences with the professor, at his initiation and with his encouragement. Because he was so self-disclosing in class, and because we were supposed to relate what we were reading to our own experiences, I shared my feelings with him. His responses to my journal entries became more and more personal. In this way, I thought a rare friendship was developing with someone whose politics and commitment to ethics in education I shared. I was extremely flattered by his interest in me . . . By displacing our student-teacher relationship onto nonacademic ground, symbolically and literally, he masked the inherent power imbalance between my role as a student and his as a professor. The relationship thus seems to be one between two consenting adults. And, indeed, this professor was not a lecherous power-monger, pinning students against his desk and promising a good grade for sexual favors. He never said he desired me sexually, he never threatened me with academic retribution if I didn't submit to his demands, he was not overtly coercive . . . His pattern was to use the journal to establish a close relationship, and the political groups to increase access to women and to encourage them to think of him not as a professor but as a friend, a man. Then he would encourage any physical advances the context would allow. For me it stopped with kissing, but with one of the women [students], he engaged in [sexual] intercourse in the department lounge."*

<u>Hybrid Techniques</u>. While the five approaches described above are relatively unique and independent, some faculty sexual predators utilize a combined or hybrid strategy to exploit their prey. For example, a harasser might begin with the intellectual seducer approach and then at the right time, follow with the Gate-Keeper/Power-Broker technique, explicitly offering a passing grade or recommendation in exchange for sex.

Writing in Michele Paludi's edited book entitled, <u>Sexual Harassment on College Campuses</u>, Kathryn Quina offers a disgusting example of a harasser's hybrid strategy.

> *"When a nationally known scholar asked her to participate in his research project, Ellen was thrilled. Flattered by his attentiveness and*

excited by promises of a letter of recommendation to top graduate schools, she worked long hours, collecting data and writing up a paper herself. Shortly before it was to be sent for publication, Dr. X delivered his ultimatum: no sex, no authorship. Ellen submitted, although disgusted by him physically, because she was so invested in the project. After they had sex, he laughed at her tears. The next day, he told her he did not consider her contributions very thoughtful or important, certainly not sufficient to deserve authorship, and that he had allowed her to work on these projects only because he knew how much she wanted to be near him. Ellen lost a year of work, her chance for a good graduate placement, and two publications. More importantly, she lost her confidence. Dr. X's comments were emotionally devastating, and ultimately felt more degrading to her than the sexual acts."

Conclusions

Knowing how to identify faculty sexual predators and understanding how they operate are critical to protect yourself. Do not let anyone violate your civil rights! If you feel that a professor is trying to use one or more of the above techniques on you, try to assertively stop it before it gets started (see Chapter 6). If the predator persists, carefully collect evidence to document the harassment (see Chapter 8), and then file a formal complaint (see Chapter 7).

CHAPTER 3

What is Academic Sexual Harassment? —

Know Your Legal Rights!

Amanda was starting to feel very uncomfortable again as she was taking lecture notes in her biology course. Dr. P. had frequently brought sexually explicit pornographic materials to class and talked about them. This typically included demeaning comments about women and their role as sex objects.

Today, the professor was especially excited about a real-life slide he was about to project on the classroom screen. When he did, the room was instantly filled with gasps and exclamations. The slide depicted a pop bottle inserted into a woman's vagina! Dr. P. thought that it was hilarious and called on women students for their reactions.

Needless to say, Amanda was stunned, embarrassed, and offended by the slide and the professor's outrageous conduct. She felt something was terribly wrong. On the other hand, Dr. P. had been teaching at the university for over 20 years—so maybe his behavior was somehow acceptable.

Amanda was confused about what had happened to her and uncertain as to what action she should take. She dreaded her next biology class and finally decided to withdraw and forfeit her course tuition.

After talking with several friends, Amanda still was not certain whether the professor's behavior was prohibited or unlawful. She also did not know whether she could file a complaint, or how to file a complaint, or where to file a complaint. Amanda finally concluded that it would be pointless to try to file a complaint because the school had tolerated the professor's outrageous conduct for so long.

Amanda's experience is all too common in colleges and universities throughout the country. Although she felt strongly that the professor's behavior was wrong [it was both <u>wrong</u> and <u>unlawful</u>], she was genuinely confused by the institution's obvious willingness to condone his offensive conduct for over 20 years.

Amanda, like many other college students, was unfamiliar with sexual harassment laws and her specific rights. Thus, she did not realize that her civil rights had been clearly violated by Dr. P. and that she had multiple options concerning where to file a complaint.

Unfortunately, many universities are perfectly content to "keep students in the dark" about sexual harassment on campus. Here's why. If you don't know what your rights are, you certainly are not likely to file a complaint. If no complaints are filed, then the institution does not have a sexual harassment problem.

We have an example that perfectly illustrates this type of institutional thinking.

After the appearance of a local newspaper article concerning alleged faculty sexual assault and sexual harassment of a female student, this university requested the services of a sexual harassment consultant. The administration was very worried about continued negative publicity that might result in significant enrollment declines— especially given that 70% of the student body was female.

The consultant presented the administration with a written plan to effectively prevent sexual harassment on campus. An essential component of the plan involved mandatory educational training sessions for all students. The content would include information about student rights and how to file complaints.

After reviewing the consultant's plan, the institution's top two administrators refused to conduct any student training. They argued that if students knew what their rights were, there would be a flood of new sexual harassment complaints. The campus was already having difficulties dealing with the first complaint and did not want any additional problems. Needless to say, no student training/education was conducted.

This anecdote provides compelling evidence that you <u>cannot</u> <u>trust</u> many colleges and universities to effectively educate you about your civil rights and complaint options. You need to take <u>personal</u> <u>responsibility</u> for your own education in this area.

Our book represents an effort to help you learn as much as possible about your fundamental civil rights and how to protect them. Knowing your rights and complaint options is an essential first step in insuring that you are not victimized by sexual harassment on campus.

Quiz

Before you continue reading, take a few moments to complete the quiz on the following page. It provides a good indication of your present knowledge concerning academic sexual harassment. The answers to these questions, along with brief explanations, are provided at the end of the chapter.

Academic Sexual Harassment Quiz

<u>Circle One</u>

True   False   1.   The primary legal framework protecting
                       students from sexual harassment is Title V of
                       the 1936 Educational Rights Act.

True   False   2.   Federal law protects students against sexual
                       harassment at any educational institution that
                       receives federal funding.

True   False   3.   The Department of Education has the power to
                       sue academic institutions in court for the sexual
                       harassment of students.

True   False   4.   Students are not allowed to seek monetary
                       damages in sexual harassment cases against
                       educational institutions.

True   False   5.   There is no statute of limitations for filing a
                       complaint of sexual harassment with the
                       Department of Education.

True   False   6.   If a student voluntarily consents to a sexual
                       relationship with a professor, one can legally
                       conclude that the student welcomed the
                       professor's sexual conduct.

True   False   7.   Universities are only liable for damages in
                       sexual harassment cases if their response to the
                       official complaint was deliberately indifferent.

True   False   8.   A professor who seeks sex from a student in
                       exchange for a better grade is engaged in quid
                       pro quo sexual harassment.

True   False   9.   Persistent, sexually offensive remarks by a professor in class may constitute hostile environment sexual harassment.

True   False   10.   Retaliation of any kind against someone who has filed a sexual harassment complaint is unlawful.

What is Academic Sexual Harassment?

While there is often a great deal of discussion and confusion about academic sexual harassment, one point is of paramount importance. Academic sexual harassment represents an <u>illegal</u> <u>violation</u> of a student's <u>civil</u> <u>rights</u> and a <u>clear</u> <u>abuse</u> of a <u>professor's</u> <u>power</u> and <u>authority</u>.

There are basically two types of academic sexual harassment. The first is known as "quid pro quo" (a Latin phrase meaning "this for that"), while the second is called hostile environment.

<u>Quid Pro Quo</u>. This type of harassment typically involves a faculty member who makes an unwanted offer of a tangible academic benefit (test score, project grade, course grade, thesis approval, letter of recommendation, etc.) to a student in exchange for sexual favors. See Figure 3-1.

Figure 3-1

Elements of Quid Pro Quo Sexual Harassment

1. an unwelcome sexual advance by the professor toward the student

2. the student's decision to accept or reject the professor's advance is used to make an academic decision about her (test scores, grades, thesis approval, letter of recommendation, etc.)

Some faculty predators are very brazen in committing quid pro quo harassment. In one instance, an undergraduate student was asked to come to the professor's office, where he proceeded to inform her "if she wanted to pass the course, she would have to sleep with him"!

Other faculty members are more subtle and discreet when approaching women students. They suggest that participating together in various sexual activities could be mutually satisfying and beneficial. This can be translated as "you will get a better grade"!

When evaluating sexual harassment cases (both quid pro quo and hostile environment discussed below), it is important to review federal guidelines that address the issue of welcomeness. In other words, did the student welcome the professor's advances or not. The suggestion is that unlawful harassment only occurs when a professor's conduct is unwelcome by the student.

Faculty sexual harassers are often quick to defend their behavior by arguing that the student welcomed their advances, or perhaps even solicited them. Experts in the field and many universities reject this reasoning and focus accountability squarely on the professor.

Given the tremendous power differential between students and faculty, it is clearly the professor's responsibility to appropriately manage all interaction with students to insure that sexual conduct and exploitation do not occur. This professional standard applies to all students, including those who welcome or appear to welcome a professor's advances.

Indiana University specifically addresses this topic in its academic handbook for faculty members.

> "Faculty members exercise power over students, whether in giving them praise or criticism, evaluating them, making recommendations for their further studies or their future employment, or conferring any other benefits on them. All amorous or sexual relationships between faculty members and students are unacceptable when the faculty member has any professional responsibility for the student [emphasis added]. Such situations greatly increase the chances that the faculty member will abuse his or her power and sexually exploit the student. Voluntary consent by the student in such a relationship is suspect, given the fundamental asymmetric nature of the relationship [emphasis added]. Moreover, other students and faculty may be affected by such unprofessional behavior because it places the faculty member in a position to favor or advance one student's interest at the expense of others and implicitly makes obtaining benefits contingent on amorous or sexual favors. Therefore, the University will view it as a violation of this Code of Academic Ethics if faculty members engage in amorous or sexual relations with students for whom they have professional

responsibility, even when both parties have consented or appear to have consented to the relationship. Such professional responsibility encompasses both instructional and non-instructional contexts."

Quid pro quo is considered to be the most blatant form of academic sexual harassment. It clearly represents an illegal abuse of a professor's power and authority over their student.

Hostile Environment. The second type of harassment typically involves a pattern of unwelcome sexually offensive comments/behaviors on the part of a professor that is unrelated to course content and (1) interferes with a student's academic performance or (2) is perceived by the student as threatening, intimidating, and/or offensive. The same comments made about "welcomeness" above apply to hostile environment harassment. See Figure 3-2.

Figure 3-2

Elements of Hostile Environment Sexual Harassment

1.   a pattern of unwelcome sexual comments/behaviors by the professor in a given class

2.   the professor's sexual comments/behaviors are unrelated to course content

3.   the professor's sexual comments/behaviors interfere with the student's academic performance and/or

4.   the professor's sexual comments/behaviors are perceived by the student as threatening, intimidating, and/or offensive.

For example, the anecdote about Amanda at the beginning of this chapter represents a clear illustration of unlawful hostile environment sexual harassment. Recall that the professor frequently brought pornographic materials to class and made demeaning comments about women as sex objects. His outrageous behavior culminated with the deplorable pop-bottle slide.

The professor's conduct was obviously unwelcomed and interfered with Amanda's academic performance—she ultimately dropped the class. In addition, Amanda felt threatened, intimidated and offended by the faculty member's actions. Clearly, she was victimized by sexual harassment. Her fundamental civil rights were violated and she had a compelling basis for filing a complaint.

As we mentioned earlier, hostile environment harassment usually involves a pattern of repeated sexually offensive comments/behaviors. However, in some cases, a single event is serious enough to create a hostile learning environment.

For example, at one university, Sue made an appointment to visit a professor's office to discuss her grade on a recent test. When she knocked on his office door, he told her to come in. Upon entering, Sue was immediately confronted by the professor who had his pants pulled down and exposed himself to her. She shrieked and immediately ran from the office down the hallway.

Sue refused to attend another class with this professor and was deeply offended by his conduct. In this instance, the professor's conduct was so outrageous or egregious that the single event was sufficient to create a hostile learning environment.

<u>Reasonable Person or Reasonable Woman Standard</u>. A critically important element in hostile environment harassment is the student's perception that the professor's comments/behaviors are threatening, intimidating, and/or offensive. When resolving sexual harassment cases, courts utilize a "reasonable person" or "reasonable woman" standard in determining whether a faculty member's comments/behaviors were sufficiently severe as to be unlawful.

In other words, would a "reasonable person" or "reasonable woman" view the professor's sexual comments/behaviors as seriously threatening, intimidating, and/or offensive? Thus, a woman student must be prepared to demonstrate that the professor's sexual conduct was objectionable to her as well as any "reasonable person" or "reasonable woman".

The pop-bottle slide mentioned earlier in this chapter represents an action that would easily meet the "reasonable person" or "reasonable woman" standard. The same applies to the professor who exposed himself to a student.

Examples of Potentially Illegal Sexual Harassment

Professors can be very creative when developing new ways to sexually harass and exploit female students. Thus, it is impossible to develop a list of every potentially illegal action on their part.

Figure 3-3 provides a listing of techniques commonly used by faculty sexual predators to harass women students.

Figure 3-3

Examples of Potentially Illegal Sexual Harassment

Verbal: Sexual innuendos, suggestive comments, insulting/vulgar/lewd remarks, jokes of a sexual nature, requests for dates, sexual propositions, and threats.

Nonverbal: Sexually suggestive objects, posters, photos, cartoons, or graffiti, suggestive or insulting sounds, leering, whistling, and obscene gestures.

Physical: Unwelcome physical contact, including touching, pinching, petting, brushing against one's body, fondling, and sexual activities.

Legal Framework

The current legal framework for academic sexual harassment can be found in three major federal statutes. They include:

(1)   Title VII of the Civil Rights Act of 1964,

(2)   Title IX of the Educational Amendment of 1972 to the Civil Rights Act of 1964, and,

(3)   the Civil Rights Act of 1991.

We will briefly identify the major provisions of each of these statutes.

Title VII of the Civil Rights Act of 1964. This statute pertains specifically to workplace discrimination. However, it has also served as the foundation for defining and resolving sexual harassment issues in academic settings.

It is important to note that if you were sexually harassed while performing duties as a part-time or full-time university employee, Title VII applies directly to your case.

Major provisions of the law and subsequent regulatory action include the following:

- Prohibits employment discrimination as a function of sex, among other factors.
- Created the Equal Employment Opportunity Commission (EEOC) as the enforcement agency for Title VII.
- The Equal Employment Opportunity Commission (1980) issued specific guidelines defining illegal sexual harassment in the workplace that apply to organizations with 15 or more employees. (These guidelines have been extended by the courts to include academic settings.)
- Harassment on the basis of sex is a violation of Sec. 703 of Title VII (of the 1964 Civil Rights Act). Unwelcome sexual advances, requests for sexual favors, and other verbal or physical conduct of a sexual nature constitute sexual harassment when:

  (1)   submission to such conduct is made either explicitly or implicitly a term or condition of an individual's employment,

  (2)   submission to or rejection of such conduct by an individual is used as the basis for employment decisions affecting such individual, or

(3)   such conduct has the purpose or effect of unreasonably interfering with an individual's work performance or creating an intimidating, hostile, or offensive working environment.
Note: (1) and (2) above involve what is known as "quid pro quo" sexual harassment (this for that). (3) above involves what is known as "hostile environment" sexual harassment.

Title IX of the Education Amendment of 1972. This federal statute provides the specific legal framework for addressing sexual discrimination within academic settings. Major provisions include:

- Prohibits sex discrimination at educational institutions receiving federal funding. Specifically, "no person in the United States shall, on the basis of sex, be excluded from participation in, be denied the benefits of, or be subjected to discrimination under any educational program or activity receiving federal financial assistance." (No specific reference to sexual harassment is made.)
- Requires that educational institutions have established grievance procedures to process complaints involving sex discrimination.
- Established the Office for Civil Rights (OCR) within the Department of Education as the enforcement agency. The OCR provides a general definition of sexual harassment as "verbal or physical conduct of sexual nature imposed on the basis of sex, by an employee or agent (professor and/or administrator) of a recipient that denies, limits, provides different, or conditions the provision of aid, benefits, services or treatment protected under Title IX." Complaints must be filed with the OCR within 180 days of the harassment in question, or within 60 days of the completion of an internal university investigation.
- Empowered the OCR to punish offending uncooperative educational institutions by requesting that their federal funding be terminated.
- Important specific OCR guidelines/definitions include the following:

    (1)   Quid Pro Quo Harassment: A school employee explicitly or implicitly conditions a student's

participation in an education program, an activity, or bases an educational decision on the student's submission to unwelcome sexual advances, request for sexual favors, or other verbal, nonverbal, or physical conduct of a sexual nature. In other words, quid pro quo harassment is the exchange of one thing for something else. For example, when a professor threatens to fail a student unless the student agrees to date the professor. Quid pro quo harassment is equally unlawful whether the student resists and suffers the threatened harm or submits and thus avoids the threatened harm.

(2)   Hostile Environment Sexual Harassment: Sexually harassing conduct that is so severe, persistent, or pervasive that it affects a student's ability to participate in or benefit from an education program or activity, or creates an intimidating, threatening or abusive educational environment. Unwelcome sexual advances, request for sexual favors, and other verbal, nonverbal, or physical conduct of a sexual nature by an employee, another student, or by a third party are all forms of hostile environment harassment.

(3)   Welcomeness: In order to be actionable as harassment, sexual conduct must be unwelcome. Conduct is unwelcome if the student did not request or invite it and "regarded the conduct as undesirable or offensive."

Participation by a student in sexual activity with a university employee or the failure to complain does not always mean that the conduct was welcome. For example, a student may decide not to resist sexual advances of a professor or may not file a complaint out of fear. Furthermore, a student may not object to a pattern of sexually demeaning comments directed at him or her by another student out of a concern that objections might cause the harasser to make more comments. The fact that a student may have accepted the conduct does not mean that he or she welcomed it. Also, the fact that a student willingly participated in conduct on one or more occasions does not prevent him or her from indicating that the same conduct has become unwelcome on a subsequent occasion. On the other hand, if a student actively participates in sexual banter and discussions and gives no indication that he or she objects, then the evidence generally will not support a conclusion that the conduct was unwelcome.

(4) Applicability of Title IX: It is important to recognize that Title IX's prohibition of sexual harassment does not extend to legitimate nonsexual touching or other nonsexual conduct. For example, a demonstration of a sports maneuver or technique requiring contact with another person will not be considered sexual harassment.

Title IX protects any "person" from sex discrimination; accordingly both male and female students are protected from sexual harassment initiated in by a school's employees, other students, or third parties. Moreover, Title IX prohibits sexual harassment regardless of the sex of the harasser, i.e., even if the harasser and the person being harassed are members of the same sex.

Civil Rights Act of 1991. This federal law provided additional significant damage awards for victims (including students) of sexual harassment and made it easier to win cases. Relevant provisions include:

- Allows victims (including students) claiming intentional sexual harassment to seek compensatory and punitive damages with monetary caps based upon employer/university size.
- Allows victims (including students) to request trial by jury (in many cases, juries are more sympathetic to student complaints than judges are).

Important Legal Developments and Concepts

Since the passage of Title IX in 1972, there have been a number of important legal developments affecting sexual harassment in academic settings.

Some of the most important developments and emerging concepts are discussed below.

1. In 1979, the Supreme Court ruled that an individual could initiate a private lawsuit against an educational institution for violation of Title IX.

2. In 1980, a U.S. Circuit Court ruled that quid pro quo harassment was a form of illegal sex discrimination as defined by Title IX.

3. In 1992, the Supreme Court ruled that students could recover monetary damages under Title IX for sexual harassment and that hostile environment sexual harassment was prohibited under Title IX. After that ruling, there was a tremendous increase in litigation against universities.

4. Courts have consistently relied on the basic principles developed within the framework of Title VII (employment discrimination) and the 1980 EEOC Guidelines on Sexual Harassment when deciding Title IX cases involving academic institutions.

5. Courts have generally held professors in academic settings to a higher or stricter standard of conduct than supervisors in employment settings. One judge wrote in 1984 that, "university professors occupy an important place in our society and have concomitant ethical obligations."

6. Apparent voluntary consent and participation by a student in a sexual relationship with a faculty member does not legally imply that the student welcomes the professor's sexual conduct. Unwelcome sexual conduct is illegal and can serve as the basis of a lawsuit.

7. Persistent, sexual offensive remarks by a professor in class may constitute hostile environment sexual harassment. Such a charge is strengthened if the comments are not germane to course subject matter.

8. Favoritism or non-participant sexual harassment involves a situation in which a student receives preferential academic treatment (grades, internships, grants, thesis approval) from a professor on the basis of her sexual relationship with him. Other students can be unfairly disadvantaged by this action and could legitimately file a complaint.

For example, Dr. T. told his graduate class that the top performing students would have an opportunity to attend a prestigious national conference and meet prospective employers. One of the students in the class, Linda, was openly dating Dr. T. and enjoyed a special relationship with him. Although she was a good student, several others in the class consistently did better on tests and projects. Unfortunately, at the conclusion of the semester, Dr. T. chose Linda to attend the conference. In this situation, the other students who had outperformed her in class were victims of favoritism or non-participant sexual harassment.

9. In all likelihood, harassment that is not sexual in nature, but nonetheless directed at only one gender would be considered illegal under Title IX. For instance, if a professor repeatedly made disparaging remarks about women's intellectual, academic, and classroom capabilities, female students could bring action against him for sex-based harassment, as originally defined by the EEOC.

10. Retaliation of any kind against someone who has filed a sexual harassment complaint is against the law.

11. Courts have traditionally been reluctant to interfere with or overrule university disciplinary procedures in sexual harassment cases. However, in one recent case, a U.S. Court of Appeals ruled that the institution violated the professor's right to free speech by enforcing an unconstitutionally vague sexual harassment policy and disciplining the instructor. The university is appealing the decision.

12. Two universities in 1996 (William and Mary and Virginia Commonwealth University) initiated lawsuits against individual faculty members found guilty of sexual harassment, claiming that the professors were personally liable for any damage awards, not the institutions.

13. Students can be held responsible and disciplined for sexually harassing other students or faculty members. Thus, <u>everyone</u> on campus has a responsibility to respect your civil rights.

14. Educational institutions can be held liable for the harassment of students and/or faculty that is caused by other students.

15. In June 1998, the Supreme Court ruled that educational institutions are <u>not</u> financially liable for damages to student victims of sexual harassment unless a senior administrator

who has authority to do something about the problem has been officially notified and is "<u>deliberately indifferent</u>" to the harassment. This ruling underscores the importance of filing formal complaints against harassers in order to properly notify institutions of the unlawful behavior.

Unfortunately, however, as you might suspect, it is very difficult to prove that a school's response to a complaint was "deliberately indifferent", if some action, regardless of how insignificant, was taken. Efforts are underway to pass federal legislation to override this "deliberate indifference" requirement and provide better protection and legal recourse for students.

Currently, as long as institutions have some response to a complaint, they can easily demonstrate that they were not "deliberately indifferent." Thus, there is no incentive to deal aggressively and more effectively with faculty sexual predators and compensate victims.

Until favorable legislation is passed, we offer the following suggestion to victims of sexual harassment and their attorneys. Most faculty sexual predators are serial harassers, with a long history of violating student civil rights. If prior complaints have been filed against the professor who harassed you, there is a strong possibility that he received, at best, a slap-on-the-wrist punishment from the university. He might even have an extensive record of multiple relatively minor disciplinary actions. From our perspective, placing a serial harasser back in the college classroom, knowing that he will likely harass again, demonstrates brazen "deliberate indifference" for the civil rights of students. We encourage plaintiffs to use this logic when it applies to their situation and we challenge universities to defend this despicable practice. We're confident that juries would side with students!

Conclusions

Before you go or return to college, make sure you know exactly what constitutes sexual harassment and what your civil rights are! Remember, your fundamental civil rights include the right to attend college in an environment free of sexual harassment! Knowing your rights is the first step in protecting them.

If you are uncertain or confused about any issue related to sexual harassment, contact one of the following: (1) your institution's Student Advocate/Ombudsperson or (2) the Office for Civil Rights of the U.S. Department of Labor— regional office addresses and telephone numbers are listed in Appendix A on Selected References and Resources. If you are ready to file a complaint, see Chapter 7 for our advice on this process.

Correct Answers to
Academic Sexual Harassment Quiz

1.	False	The primary legal framework that protects students from sexual harassment is Title IX of the Educational Amendment of 1972.
2.	True	Title IX of the Educational Amendment of 1972 protects students against sex discrimination (including sexual harassment) at any educational institution that receives federal funding.
3.	False	Title IX of the Educational Amendment of 1972 does not permit the Department of Education to sue academic institutions in court for sexual harassment of students. Instead, the Department of Education can punish offending institutions by requesting that their federal funding be terminated.
4.	False	Federal law and Supreme Court rulings allow students to seek monetary damages in sexual harassment cases against educational institutions.
5.	False	There is a statute of limitations for filing a complaint of sexual harassment with the Department of Education. Complaints must be filed within 180 days of the harassment in question, or within 60 days of the completion of an internal university investigation.
6.	False	Apparent voluntary consent and participation by a student in a sexual relationship with a faculty member does not legally imply that the student welcomes the professor's sexual conduct.
7.	True	After a Supreme Court ruling in 1998, universities are only liable for damages in sexual harassment cases if they were officially notified and their response was deemed "deliberately indifferent".

8.   True   A professor who seeks sex from a student in exchange for a better grade is engaged in quid pro quo sexual harassment.

9.   True   Persistent, sexually offensive remarks by a professor in class may constitute hostile environment sexual harassment.

10.   True   Retaliation of any kind against someone who has filed a sexual harassment complaint is unlawful.

Interpretation

If you scored 7 out of 10 or higher, you already have a solid understanding of academic sexual harassment and what your rights are. However, unless you scored a perfect 10, there are still things for you to learn about these issues. Hopefully, the material in this book will help you improve. Good luck!

CHAPTER 4

The Lecherous University in Operation—

Women Beware!

After filing a sexual harassment complaint against an English faculty member at the University of Pennsylvania, the victim uncovered some very disturbing information. This professor had previously taught at Bates College in Maine, where students had also accused him of sexual harassment. Bates allowed him to leave quietly in 1991, with positive recommendations that helped him obtain the position at the University of Pennsylvania. The young woman involved filed civil lawsuits against: (1) the faculty member for sexually harassing her, (2) Penn for allowing the sexual harassment to occur and negligent hiring, and (3) Bates for failing to reveal the reasons why the professor left (Time Magazine, April 3, 1995).

The above incident vividly portrays the extraordinary accommodations that universities extend to faculty sexual predators, at the obvious expense of students. Rather than appropriately disciplining or terminating a professor for sexually harassing coeds, many institutions prefer a cowardly, dishonest course of action. Simply ask the offender to resign and provide glowing letters of reference to help him find a position at another university. Absolutely unconscionable!

The purpose of this chapter is to help you understand how universities operate in ways that foster a sexually permissive climate for faculty and deprive students of their civil and consumer rights. Armed with this knowledge, we hope that you can more effectively prevent and combat sexual harassment on campus.

Pro-Faculty Bias

One overriding factor is essential to understanding how institutions of higher education function in the United States. Simply put, universities are organized and operated primarily for the benefit of faculty members, especially tenured ones, as we will discuss below. The plain truth is that faculty come first!

Everyone else, including students and their parents, is of considerably less importance.

Furthermore, since the vast majority of college professors (and administrators as well) are men, universities tend to vigorously protect and defend the interests of male professors. All of this works to the decided disadvantage of students, especially women.

In order to fully comprehend how and why institutions of higher education operate as they do, three prominent characteristics of university systems are particularly important: tenure, academic freedom, and faculty governance. While each of these topics is complex and multifaceted, we will try to demystify them and show how they contribute to the sexual harassment problem on campus.

Tenure. Tenure originated in medieval times as a way to protect professors from capricious job dismissals as a result of philosophical, political, or religious views that differed from the prevailing norms on campus or in society at large. The goal was to encourage the free expression of ideas, regardless of how unconventional or radical they might seem.

In its present form, professors with tenure are virtually guaranteed lifetime employment. This guarantee extends to faculty who are incompetent, unproductive, and unresponsive to students. More ominously, it also protects faculty sexual predators from appropriate discipline in most instances and essentially assures that they will not be fired, even for serious or repeated offenses. Outrageous, isn't it!

Here's how the tenure process works. Newly hired professors are typically given a 6-year probationary period, during which they demonstrate their performance excellence in the areas of teaching, research, and service. During their sixth year of employment, professors are required to assemble a "tenure file" documenting their performance achievements. The "tenure file" is then submitted to various faculty committees (often consisting predominately of male tenured professors) for review, as well as to academic administrators (more often than not, also male tenured professors) in the individual's "chain of command". If granted tenure, a professor can be confident of lifetime employment with that institution. If tenure is denied, a professor's position is terminated and she/he has one year to find a new job.

The tenure file review process is hopelessly subjective and grossly inconsistent with human resource management professional standards for performance appraisal. However, the subjectivity allows reviewers to deny tenure to any professor who may be a woman or who may represent a challenge to the "good-old-boy network" of harassers and their supporters. Thus, the tenure process protects those in power and perpetuates the status quo—an academic environment that strongly favors men and their interests at the expense of women. In terms of campus sexual harassment, this means that once tenured, faculty sexual predators know that there is very little likelihood that they will ever lose their jobs, regardless of how often or how seriously they violate student civil rights.

Academic Freedom. Academic freedom guarantees professors nearly unlimited latitude to say and do whatever they want to in their classrooms and courses. Together with tenure, academic freedom was originally intended to encourage the open expression and discussion of diverse ideas in the university environment, including those that deviated from prevailing norms.

Unfortunately, faculty sexual predators have utilized academic freedom as a license to harass their students. Professors often do this by creating a sexually charged classroom environment that is hostile, offensive, and intimidating to women and interferes with learning. Another common tactic is to engage in an ongoing attack on women students by degrading, belittling, and denigrating them in class.

When confronted, harassers immediately invoke academic freedom as a justification and defense for this reprehensible conduct. They display "righteous indignation" that anyone would dare question their classroom behavior. If a formal complaint is filed, harassers strive to position themselves as innocent victims of an illegitimate assault on academic freedom and the constitutional right to free speech, as well as valiant defenders of faculty privilege. Sadly, this twisted strategy can often generate considerable campus support among fellow professors for their "plight".

Let's be crystal clear about the relationship between academic freedom and your civil rights. Under no circumstances does academic freedom permit professors to violate your civil rights! Don't allow this to happen under any circumstances!

Faculty Governance. Faculty governance is a critically important concept in U.S. higher education. It provides professors with nearly total control of university decisions that affect academic issues. These include: (a) hiring of new faculty and administrators, (b) faculty promotion and tenure, (c) curriculum content and faculty teaching assignments, (d) faculty training and education, (e) complaint processing procedures, and (f) punishments for faculty misconduct. These will be discussed in more detail below.

As you can readily see, professors have enormous power on college campuses. More specifically, since most college professors are men, the "good-old-boy network" dominates campus operation. Their agenda and their interests receive priority attention. Unfortunately, this reality often creates conditions that foster and encourage sexual harassment of female students.

The Impact of Tenure, Academic Freedom, and Faculty Governance on University Operation

Tenure, academic freedom, and faculty governance combine to powerfully impact major aspects of university operations in ways that strongly favor faculty, at the expense of students. From our perspective, the most significant factors that result in the creation of a pro-faculty bias and lecherous climate on campus include the following.

Hiring Academic Administrators. Perhaps the most significant evidence of a pro-faculty bias is the manner in which academic administrators are selected and the characteristics of people who hold these positions. The process of hiring an administrator typically begins by forming a search committee, consisting predominantly of faculty members (the majority of whom are men).

The search committee writes the position description and newspaper ad, solicits applications and nominations, reviews and evaluates credentials, and submits a list of acceptable candidates to the appropriate campus administrator (again, most are men). In the overwhelming majority of all cases, someone is hired from this approved list of candidates. Very, very rarely will an administrator overrule the recommendations of the faculty search committee and hire another person. Such an act of heresy would be the "kiss of death" as an administrator and lead to an early end to one's career.

What are the characteristics of academic administrators hired using this process? The answer may depress you. First, notice that we have not used the term leader, but instead have chosen administrator. With very few exceptions, individuals who hold these positions are not leaders and will never be leaders. They are selected as caretakers to simply administer an organizational system that preserves and protects the rights of male faculty members. Their specific characteristics include:

1. A strong record of active support for faculty rights and privileges. This support must be clearly dominant over any concerns about student interests.

2. A demonstrated willingness to accept direction from campus faculty and follow their lead.

3. A lack of courage in taking positions that oppose faculty interests, even when student civil rights are involved.

4. A blind commitment to preserve the tenure system and protect tenured faculty members, regardless of how offensive or egregious their conduct is.

5. A moral compass that is situationally defined by what is best for faculty members, not students or anyone else.

6. No record of appropriately disciplining faculty for misconduct, especially sexual harassment; and no inclination to do so in the future.

7. Male with tenure.

8. Many times, a prior history of exploitative sexual and romantic relationships with students.

Regrettably, aspiring administrators with the above qualifications have a bright future in academia. Without these characteristics, candidates have little chance of being selected for an administrative position or succeeding if hired. Writing in Forbes magazine (September 7, 1998), Dr. Thomas Sowell, an economist and senior fellow at the Hoover Institute expresses agreement with the following assertion, " . . . using search committees to pick university presidents virtually guarantees that people with convictions and backbone [emphasis added] will be passed over in favor of people who don't rub any campus constituencies the wrong way." We fully concur with this viewpoint!

The example that follows, along with the others in this book, illustrates the enormous role that university administrators play in the horrible problem of sexual harassment on campus.

(The Daily News, Hopkinsville, KY, April 2, 1999).
"Western Kentucky University disregarded recommendations to fire an administrator accused of sexual harassment by more than 50 women, according to internal documents. The documents also indicate that some administrators interfered in the investigation . . ."

How could this serial harasser continue to be employed at a state university? How could his offenses go unpunished? How could the institution continue to put women students at risk and jeopardize their civil rights? The answers to these questions can be found in the academic administrator characteristics we discussed above!

Faculty Discipline. When a sexual harassment complaint is filed against a professor, the case is typically presented to a faculty hearing committee (consisting primarily of tenured male professors). This committee evaluates evidence, renders a decision about guilt or innocence, and when someone is found guilty, recommends an "appropriate" punishment for the offender. This process is discussed in more detail in Chapter 7.

Can you conceive of a way to "stack the deck" more heavily in favor of the accused professor? In all likelihood his colleagues, buddies, and supporters are represented on the hearing committee. They have a personal vested interest in protecting "one of their own"; and who knows, the next complaint might be filed against one of them. The guiding principle is "you scratch my back, and I'll scratch yours." If student civil rights get violated and revilolated in the process, that's too bad.

If by some chance a faculty hearing committee does recommend punishment for a convicted harasser, the recommendations are forwarded to a spineless, complacent administrator (also typically a tenured male professor) and generally fail to even constitute a "slap-on-the-wrist".

An education professor admitted to stalking and sexually propositioning a graduate student. The faculty hearing committee recommended that he receive a letter of reprimand and suggested that he seek counseling. Of course, the pro-faculty administrator wholeheartedly concurred and "imposed the sentence"! A few years later, the same professor admitted to fondling a young high school girl visiting campus in the summer. His "punishment", another letter of reprimand and a requirement that he seek counseling—although this never occurred. The professor remained on the faculty until a young woman had the courage to file criminal charges against him for sexual assault. At that point, a "caring and supportive" administrator successfully encouraged him to take early retirement.

In our opinion, the utter lack of serious disciplinary consequences (including termination) for egregious and repeated acts of sexual harassment and assault demonstrates brazen disregard for student civil rights. Allowing convicted faculty sexual predators to continue to prey on unsuspecting women students is unconscionable! We also believe that this behavior more than meets the "deliberate indifference" standard that the Supreme Court (see Chapter 3) has defined for determining if institutions can be held liable in sexual harassment cases.

Serial harassers should not be allowed to hold positions as professors. Institutions who permit this to occur should be held fully accountable. We encourage women who have been victimized by convicted predators to aggressively pursue universities for damages using this logic.

Worse than a "slap-on-the-wrist", some institutions actually "reward" professors for sexual harassment.

At one university, a professor who admitted to having sex with a student was "punished" (or more accurately, rewarded) with a suspension from teaching responsibilities for an entire semester—at full pay. Following this, the joke among fellow harassers and their supporters on campus was—"bag a coed and get an automatic, paid, semester-long vacation."

Disclosure of Disciplinary Records. While a variety of programs are currently available at the state or national level to provide consumers with information about the disciplinary records of such professionals as attorneys, physicians, clergy, counselors, and stockbrokers, universities vigorously resist any such efforts to make faculty discipline records available to students. Why? It is not in the best interest of professors, especially faculty sexual predators who have a record to hide.

Would such information be useful and valuable to students and their parents? Of course it would, but without tremendous external pressure, pro-faculty universities will never voluntarily provide this data.

Public Dissemination of Harassment Incidence Rates. The staggering problem of academic sexual harassment is one of the best-kept, dirty secrets of higher education in our country. The public is generally unaware that the problem exists and certainly has no idea of its magnitude or horrible impact on victims. The reason is clear and compelling. It is not in the best interests of university faculty members to have this type of information disseminated to the public, regardless of the continuing damage done to students. That might upset the status quo; invite further scrutiny, or worst still, possible regulation. In our opinion, powerful external pressure is needed to force institutions to release this type of data.

Faculty Hiring Decisions. Just as faculty search committees evaluate and recommend candidates for administrative positions, the same basic process is used in hiring professors. Once again, male-dominated search committees make their highly subjective recommendations to predominantly male administrators. Is it any wonder then that candidates who happen to be women or those that support equal employment opportunity, student rights, or other issues at odds with the "good-old-boy-network" are rarely hired. This perpetuates the status quo and further solidifies faculty rights and privileges at the expense of everything else.

Faculty Tenure Decisions. As discussed above, faculty committees (composed principally of tenured males) evaluate tenure files submitted by professors in their sixth year of employment and make recommendations to university administrators (also typically tenured males) about the final decision. Only infrequently do administrators override committee recommendations.

The net impact of this process is to deny tenure to outspoken women or anyone espousing views that pose a threat to the male dominated status quo. Critics of the pro-male bias in higher education are rarely tenured. Instead they are forced to seek employment elsewhere and start the process over again, from the beginning.

Other Important Decisions Affecting Professors. In addition to discipline and tenure, faculty committees, dominated by men, make virtually binding recommendations on a wide range of academic decisions that have a substantial impact on the lives of professors. These include: (a) promotions, (b) sabbaticals—every seven years, a semester off at full pay or an academic year off at half-pay, to concentrate on an important project, (c) raises, (d) campus grants for research support, and (e) teaching assignments.

These issues continue to be significant to professors throughout their academic careers. Harassers and the "good-old-boy-network" use this considerable leverage to stifle campus criticism and reform efforts and intimidate anyone who speaks out against them.

For example, the first author of this book was told, off the record, by a senior campus administrator that he would never be promoted to full professor, regardless of how stellar his performance. His aggressive efforts to prevent sexual harassment and punish offenders were viewed as a serious threat to the status quo and inconsistent with professional collegiality. Harassers, their supporters, the "good-old-boy-network", and administrators all expressed outrage at the lack of respect for faculty rights and privileges and the "zealous" support for student civil and consumer rights.

Conclusions

Hopefully, the material in this chapter will help you better understand how and why higher education institutions operate as they do. The predominant organizing principle is a pervasive pro-faculty bias that infects virtually every aspect of university life. All of this comes at the considerable expense of students, especially women striving for an education in a male-dominated setting that allows sexual harassment to flourish.

Comprehending how universities function should help you in both preventing and attacking the problem. The culprit is clear, our real challenge is to devise strategies to combat the pro-male bias and eliminate sexual harassment on campus!

CHAPTER 5

How Lecherous is Your University

"Indiana University Chancellor Resigns Amid Harassment Charges" (article in The Chronicle of Higher Education, 23 Jun 95, Personal and Professional section, page A15).

"The chancellor at Indiana University's South Bend campus has resigned amid accusations that he sexually harassed a female employee. But he has been granted a one-year paid sabbatical in academic 1995-96 and will return to the faculty as a tenured professor of physics after that.

Lynn Fall, coordinator of off-campus programs for the South Bend campus, complained that the former chancellor, H. Daniel Cohen, physically attacked her, touching her sexually while she was talking to him in his office last year.

In an interview last week, she said the university had failed to punish Mr. Cohen for his behavior. "They have cut him a very sweet deal," she said. "He's on a paid vacation." Mr. Cohen will earn his $110,000 salary while he is on leave next year and will be paid $91,600 as a professor."

"Former University Chancellor Owes $805,000 in Harassment Suit" (article in Educator's Guide to Controlling Sexual Harassment, Monthly Bulletin, November 1998, p. 5)

"A federal jury in early October ordered a former Indiana University chancellor to pay a former university employee $805,157 in damages for sexual harassment she allegedly endured from him. Although the university also was found liable for the harassment, the jury awarded no damages against the school.

Former employee Lynn Fall in 1996 sued former chancellor Daniel Cohen and the university, saying they were liable for an incident in which Cohen allegedly called Fall into his office, grabbed her "like a gorilla," kissed her and groped her breasts.

> After the incident, Cohen, who denied the allegations, was forced to resign as chancellor but was permitted to continue working as a physics professor.
>
> Ultimately, the jury found the university liable but awarded zero damages against it. As to the claims against Cohen, it found against him on both the battery and the harassment claims. The jury awarded* $400,000 in *punitive* damages for each claim and $5,157 in compensatory damages for both claims. (**Fall v. Indiana University Board of Trustees**, N.D., Ind., No. 3:96-CV-205, Oct. 2, 1998)"

Unfortunately, the above incident is typical of the way most universities deal with sexual harassment and raises several disturbing questions. How can an institution allow an individual to teach undergraduate classes who has been forced to resign as campus chancellor and convicted of sexual harassment in a federal court? Doesn't this conduct demonstrate a brazen disregard for student civil and consumer rights? How can a university president and board of trustees display such cowardly leadership in failing to dismiss the convicted harasser, regardless of his tenure status?

The purpose of this chapter is to help you and your parents in the search for a university that is serious about protecting your civil and consumer rights. We will introduce a bill of rights for both students and the parents concerning faculty sexual harassment/sexual misconduct and share preliminary research results. We will also share with you the findings of two surveys we conducted concerning sexual harassment in higher education. Finally, we will preview a comprehensive evaluation tool that we have developed to assess university efforts to prevent sexual harassment on campus.

Bill of Rights

After grappling with the problem of academic sexual harassment for over 20 years, we are convinced that a critical element in any comprehensive solution involves guaranteeing students and their parents a set of essential rights. In other words, a bill of rights for consumers of higher education, similar to that legislated recently for medical patients.

We have developed a set of these essential rights for both college students and their parents, specifically concerning faculty sexual harassment/sexual misconduct. We feel that these documents cover all of the vital issues necessary to successfully combat the problem. If we've missed something from your perspective, please let us know.

Students. Our 16-item Student Bill of Rights is provided in Figure 5-1. It addresses the major areas of: (a) prevention, (b) education, (c) treatment of victims, (d) discipline for faculty sexual predators, and (e) publication of harassment incidence statistics. We strongly believe that universities have a legal, moral, and professional responsibility to guarantee and aggressively protect these fundamental student civil and consumer rights.

Parents. From our perspective, parents of college students are also important consumers of higher education. They often save and sacrifice for many years to send their children to school. Consequently, we formulated a Parent Bill of Rights concerning faculty sexual harassment/sexual misconduct, which is patterned after the one for students. It is presented in Figure 5-2. Once again, we feel that universities have a compelling responsibility to honor and respect these parental rights.

Figure 5-1

College Students Bill of Rights
Concerning Faculty Sexual Harassment/Sexual Misconduct

All college/university students should be guaranteed the following rights
concerning faculty sexual harassment/sexual misconduct:

1.   The right to receive and review, prior to enrolling at a
      college/university, published summary statistics on the incidence
      of documented faculty sexual harassment/sexual misconduct
      cases on campus.

2.   The right to attend classes, receive academic
      advising/counseling, and participate in any college/university
      related activity in an environment free of faculty sexual
      harassment/sexual misconduct.

3.   The right to be led by campus administrators (department heads,
      deans, and presidents) who do not have past histories involving
      unpublicized or unreported sexual harassment/sexual misconduct
      that prevent them from aggressively protecting student rights.

4.   The right to receive mandatory education/training on faculty
      sexual harassment/sexual misconduct to include:
      a.   a clear statement of student rights and
            responsibilities,
      b.   specific guidelines concerning appropriate and
            inappropriate faculty behaviors,
      c.   simple instructions concerning how and where to file
            a complaint, and

> d.   a full explanation of options to initiate civil and/or criminal charges, along with applicable filing deadlines.

5.   The right to be taught, advised, and counseled by faculty members who have successfully completed a <u>mandatory</u> education/training program on sexual harassment/sexual misconduct, to include:
>   a.   specific faculty responsibilities,
>   b.   clear guidelines concerning appropriate and inappropriate behaviors, and
>   c.   the serious disciplinary consequences for those who violate student rights.

6.   The <u>right</u> to know, before taking a class or selecting an advisor, whether the professor has a disciplinary record for past sexual harassment/sexual misconduct involving students.

7.   The <u>right</u> to have a truly student-friendly complaint process, complete with trained student advocates.

8.   The <u>right</u> to know that <u>all complaints</u> (both formal and informal) concerning <u>alleged</u> faculty sexual harassment/sexual misconduct will be <u>competently</u>, <u>confidentially</u>, and <u>thoroughly</u> investigated in a timely manner by qualified professionals, to include contacting <u>former students</u> who may have been victimized, or who may have information relevant to the complaint.

9.   The <u>right</u> to know that faculty <u>charged</u> with <u>serious</u> sexual harassment/sexual misconduct will be immediately removed from any positions involving student contact, pending the results of a full investigation.

10.   The <u>right</u> to know that there is student representation on any college/university board or committee charged with

hearing/reviewing cases involving faculty sexual harassment/sexual misconduct.

11. The right to know that faculty found guilty of sexual harassment/sexual misconduct will be appropriately disciplined (including suspension without pay or termination, depending upon the severity of the offense).

12. The right to receive a written apology, if victimized by faculty sexual harassment/sexual misconduct, from the college/university president.

13. The right to receive counseling/therapy, if victimized by faculty sexual harassment/sexual misconduct, paid for by the institution.

14. The right to receive a full refund of any tuition/fees paid for a course in which faculty sexual harassment/sexual misconduct occurred.

15. The right to be protected from any attempted retaliation for filing a complaint.

16. The right to know that there is student representation and input in any campus effort to publicize or address issues involving faculty sexual harassment/sexual misconduct.

Figure 5-2

Parents of College Students Bill of Rights
Concerning Faculty Sexual Harassment/Sexual Misconduct

All parents of college/university students should be guaranteed the following rights concerning faculty sexual harassment/sexual misconduct:

1. The right to receive and review, prior to the enrollment of their daughter/son at a college/university, published summary statistics on the incidence of documented faculty sexual harassment/sexual misconduct cases on campus.

2. The right to know that their daughter/son will attend classes, receive academic advising/counseling, and participate in any college/university related activity in an environment free of faculty sexual harassment/sexual misconduct.

3. The right to know that their daughter's/son's campus will be led by administrators (department heads, deans, and president) who do not have past histories involving unpublicized or unreported sexual harassment/sexual misconduct that prevent them from aggressively protecting student rights.

4. The right to know that their daughter/son will receive mandatory education/training on faculty sexual harassment/sexual misconduct to include:

    1. a clear statement of student rights and responsibilities,
    2. specific guidelines concerning appropriate and inappropriate faculty behaviors,
    3. simple instructions concerning how and where to file a complaint, and
    4. a full explanation of options to initiate civil and/or criminal charges, along with applicable filing deadlines.

5.   The <u>right</u> to know that their daughter/son will be taught, advised, and counseled by faculty members who have successfully completed a <u>mandatory</u> education/training program on sexual harassment/sexual misconduct, to include:

      1.   specific faculty responsibilities,
      2.   clear guidelines concerning appropriate and inappropriate behaviors, and
      3.   the serious disciplinary consequences for those who violate student rights.

6.   The <u>right</u> to know that, before taking a class or selecting an advisor, their daughter/son would have access to information about whether the professor has a disciplinary record for past sexual harassment/sexual misconduct involving students.

7.   The right to have a truly student-friendly complaint process, complete with trained student advocates.

8.   The <u>right</u> to know that <u>all complaints</u> (both formal or informal) concerning <u>alleged</u> faculty sexual harassment/sexual misconduct will be <u>competently</u>, <u>confidentially</u>, and <u>thoroughly</u> investigated in a timely manner by qualified professionals, to include contacting <u>former students</u> who may have been victimized, or who may have information relevant to the complaint.

9.   The <u>right</u> to know that faculty <u>charged</u> with <u>serious</u> sexual harassment/sexual misconduct will be immediately removed from any positions involving student contact, pending the results of a full investigation.

10.   The <u>right</u> to know that there is student representation on any college/university board or committee charged with hearing/reviewing cases involving faculty sexual harassment/sexual misconduct.

11. The right to know that there is representation of parents on any college/university board or committee charged with hearing/reviewing cases involving faculty sexual harassment/sexual misconduct.

12. The right to know that faculty found guilty of sexual harassment/sexual misconduct will be appropriately disciplined (including suspension without pay or termination, depending upon the severity of the offense).

13. The right to know that their daughter/son will receive a written apology, if victimized by faculty sexual harassment/sexual misconduct, from the college/university president.

14. The right to know that their daughter/son (and the entire family if necessary) will receive counseling/therapy, if victimized by faculty sexual harassment/sexual misconduct, paid for by the institution.

15. The right to know that their daughter/son will receive a full refund of any tuition/fees paid for a course in which faculty sexual harassment/sexual misconduct occurred.

16. The right to know that their daughter/son will be protected from any attempted retaliation for filing a complaint.

17. The right to know that there is student representation and input in any campus effort to publicize or address issues involving faculty sexual harassment/sexual misconduct.

18. The right to know that there is representation and input from parents in any campus effort to publicize or address issues involving faculty sexual harassment/sexual misconduct.

Preliminary Research. We have conducted preliminary consumer research with both the Student and Parent Bill of Rights. The documents were distributed to several hundred college students and their parents. Respondents were asked to rate the importance of each individual right, using a 1 (low) to 10 (high) scale.

Not surprisingly, results dramatically indicated that both students and parents considered all of the individual rights to be extremely important. Many of the parents wrote comments on their surveys indicating that they had naively assumed that these rights were already fully guaranteed by all universities. They were very shocked and dismayed to learn that this was not true.

Without a doubt, our results confirm that college students and parents highly value their rights as consumers of higher education. The challenge now is to motivate universities to meet consumer expectations and honor these rights.

Using the Bill of Rights. We encourage prospective/current college students and their parents to send these documents to presidents of the institutions they are interested in attending. Ask for a written response about each of the individual rights. Specifically, which ones will be guaranteed and which ones won't. For those that are not, request a written explanation. You have a right as a consumer to expect your university to respond to your inquiry and vigorously protect your interests. Unfortunately, our experience has been that university presidents will not even extend to you the courtesy of a response. Our advice on this matter is quite simple—if an institution fails to respond or their response is unacceptable, take your tuition dollars elsewhere!

National Mail Survey Results

The lack of emphasis on protecting student civil and consumer rights in higher education is documented in a forthcoming article in College Student Affairs Journal, entitled "Sexual Harassment Preventive and Protective Practices at U.S. Colleges and Universities", by Charles J. Hobson and Jennifer Guziewicz. A total of 536 institutions responded to our 13-item mail survey.

Among the major findings were:

1. <u>98.5%</u> (528) did not provide students with access to professors' disciplinary records concerning sexual harassment before enrolling in their classes.
2. <u>81.3%</u> (436) did not publicly report campus sexual harassment incidence statistics.
3. <u>82.3%</u> (441) did not have <u>mandatory</u> education/training programs for <u>students</u>.
4. <u>81.3%</u> (436) did not have <u>mandatory</u> education/training programs for <u>faculty</u>.
5. <u>63.6%</u> (341) did not provide any professional training for members of faculty hearing and review boards.

Clearly higher education in this country has not done an adequate job in protecting the civil and consumer rights of students. More concerted efforts are certainly needed to address this glaring deficiency.

National E-mail Survey

In preparing material for this chapter, we felt that we could provide students and their parents with helpful information by conducting a simple 2-item e-mail survey of higher educational institutions in this country. Specifically, we transmitted the message and questions contained in Figure 5-3 to the admissions office e-mail addresses of the 1,400 institutions reviewed in U.S. News and World Report's "Best Colleges in America"—2001 edition.

The two questions dealt with critically important issues covered in both the Student and Parent Bill of Rights introduced earlier. First, we were interested in whether schools currently provide prospective students with summary statistics about the incidence of campus sexual harassment. Second, we wanted to know if institutions would guarantee that no one on their teaching faculty had a prior disciplinary record for sexual harassment/sexual misconduct involving students.

Figure 5-3

University E-mail Message and 2-Item Survey

To: U.S. News and World Report's Best Colleges in America

     Admissions Offices

My name is Dr. Charles J. Hobson and I am a business professor at
Indiana University Northwest. My colleagues and I are writing a book
for prospective/current college students and their parents about sexual
harassment in higher education.

With this in mind, we have prepared a very brief, 2-item e-mail survey
(below) and are sending it to the 1,400 institutions contained in U. S.
News and World Report's "Best Colleges in America"—2001. We will
publish the results of this survey in our forthcoming book.

Could you please take a moment and answer the two questions below
and return e-mail your responses to us? Also, if your campus has
implemented any noteworthy or particularly successful programs/policies
to prevent academic sexual harassment, please share them with us!

If any questions arise, I can be reached by e-mail or phone (219) 980-
6903. Thank you in advance for your cooperation.

Survey Questions

    1.   Are summary statistics concerning the incidence of
        campus sexual harassment involving students currently
        available for review by prospective students and
        their parents?

_____ Yes (If "yes," could you please e-mail us a copy?)

_____ No

2.   Does your institution currently certify or assure prospective students and their parents that no faculty member presently teaching class has a prior disciplinary record for sexual harassment/sexual misconduct involving students?

_____ Yes

_____ No

Survey Results

Only <u>35</u> of 1,400 institutions responded to our simple e-mail survey—2.5%. The other 1,365 (97.5%) schools apparently felt that the questions we raised were not important enough to answer or they did not want to share their answers (probably "no's" to both questions) with us.

We would like to thank the 35 institutions that did respond to our survey and highlight the positive results from this sample. First, a total of four schools answered, "yes" to both questions. They do publicly report summary statistics on the incidence of campus sexual harassment and they do certify that none of their teaching faculty has a prior disciplinary record for sexual harassment/sexual misconduct involving students.

Congratulations are certainly in order for these four outstanding institutional role models (alphabetically):

ABERTUS MAGNUS COLLEGE, NEW HAVEN, CT
AQUINAS COLLEGE, GRAND RAPIDS, MI
HIRAM COLLEGE, HIRAM, OH
MCKENDREE COLLEGE, LEBANON, IL

It should be noted that: (1) in responding to Question #2 about teaching faculty with disciplinary records, the Hiram College official responding to our survey stated, "We currently have no policy in place to do this because we have NO faculty currently teaching at the College with a disciplinary record that includes a sexual harassment offense. So, while we do not certify this fact, it is indeed the case," and (2) the official from McKendree College stated that "we haven't had any charges [of sexual harassment] to report. "

Second, the following institutions publicly report sexual harassment incidence statistics and should be commended (alphabetically):

CENTRAL MICHIGAN UNIVERSITY, MT. PLEASANT, MI
COLBY COLLEGE, WATERVILLE, ME
COLLEGE OF ST. BENEDICT/ST. JOHN'S UNIVERSITY, ST. JOSEPH, MN
COLLEGE OF THE ATLANTIC, BAR HARBOR, ME
DAKOTA WESLEYAN UNIVERSITY, MITCHELL, SD
D'YOUVILLE COLLEGE, BUFFALO, NY
LYNN UNIVERSITY, BOCA RATON, FL
MILLS COLLEGE, OAKLAND, CA
MINNESOTA STATE UNIVERSITY—MANKATO, MANKATO, MN
TEMPLE UNIVERSITY, PHILADELPHIA, PA
UNIVERSITY OF MINNESOTA, MINNEAPOLIS, MN

We should point out that both Temple and the University of Minnesota have exemplary reporting formats for sexual harassment statistics. Their annual reports are available on the Web to any interested student or parent.

Third, one school responded that no one on their teaching staff had a prior disciplinary record for sexual harassment/sexual misconduct involving students.

EAST WEST UNIVERSITY, CHICAGO, IL

The school official providing answers to our survey stated, "We only certify that the faculty member has had no record while teaching at our university [excluding previous employers]."

Once again, congratulations to all of these schools for their efforts to prevent sexual harassment on campus. We hope students and their parents will take this into consideration when making enrollment decisions.

If your favorite school was not mentioned above, it is possible that our e-mail was not successfully delivered or that it was delivered to the wrong person. To rule out these possibilities, why don't you write, e-mail, or call the president or other senior administrators at your college and ask them the two questions directly. Don't be surprised if you: (1) never get answers, or (2) the answers are "No" to both questions.

Interestingly, several of the schools that did respond to our survey noted that no one had ever asked those questions before. In our opinion, until students and parents start routinely asking questions like these and holding university administrators accountable for the answers, we will not make significant progress in preventing sexual harassment on campus.

The widely publicized answers to both of our questions should be, "Yes"! If not, strongly consider spending your tuition dollars at a school with more interest in protecting your civil and consumer rights!

University Rating Scale

To assist students and their parents in evaluating how effectively institutions protect civil and consumer rights on campus, we developed the University Sexual Harassment Prevention Rating Scale (the full document is provided in Appendix B). This instrument offers a comprehensive, 100-point assessment of a university's prevention policies, programs, and practices in the following seven areas, with possible points for each one in parentheses:

1. Formal Institutional Policies (10 points)
2. Sexual Harassment Training/Education (10 points)
3. Student Support Services (10 points)
4. Complaint Processing and Investigations (15 points)
5. Complaint Resolution Outcomes for Students (5 points)
6. Faculty Discipline (25 points)
7. Public Reporting and Information Dissemination (25 points)

The points available for each of the seven areas are designed to reflect their relative importance to overall prevention success. Two examples will illustrate this point. First, groundbreaking research by Dr. Louise Fitzgerald on organizational factors that impact harassment incidence rates has clearly identified disciplinary action for offenders as critically important determinant. Without effective punishment of convicted harassers, incidence rates will soar. Thus, the Faculty Discipline factor accounts for 25 out of the total 100 points on the scale.

While most universities have strongly worded policies about protecting students from faculty harassment, very few impose appropriate disciplinary consequences on offending professors. We fully concur with Dr. Fitzgerald and believe that real progress in preventing sexual harassment on campus will not occur until academic leaders are appointed with the courage and conviction to aggressively discipline faculty sexual predators.

Our second example involves the Public Reporting and Information Dissemination Factor, which also accounts for 25 out of 100 total points on the scale. Although very few universities (only 15 of 1,400 included in the e-mail survey reported earlier in this chapter) currently provide this type of information to prospective students and their parents, we're convinced that public disclosure of harassment incidence statistics would provide a potent incentive to implement effective prevention programs on campus. Furthermore, schools with high incidence rates could expect to experience significant enrollment declines, while the reverse would be true for institutions with low rates.

Suggested Scale Use

We recommend that our comprehensive scale, or something like it, be completed annually for every university. For obvious reasons, an independent agency or organization should conduct the assessment. Possibilities include the Office for Civil Rights (OCR) of the Department of Education, existing collegiate accrediting agencies, or consumer protection organizations.

Completed annual evaluations should be made widely and publicly available. This information would allow prospective students and their parents to directly compare different institutions and chose the one that most effectively protects civil and consumer rights.

We also recommend that the scale be used in making accreditation and funding decisions. In other words, institutions that failed to achieve a designated passing score (we suggest 80% or higher) would not be accredited/reaccredited or approved for funding from state/federal government agencies or educational foundations. If actions like these were taken, universities would be forced to implement successful prevention efforts or face their inevitable demise.

Challenge to Universities

We challenge all colleges and universities in this country to voluntarily submit to an external evaluation of their harassment prevention efforts using our scale, or something like it, and publicize the results. No one would expect a school to achieve a perfect 100%. However, agreeing to the evaluation and publishing the results would provide powerful evidence of a sincere desire to identify problem areas and begin working on solutions. We would publicize your efforts in the next edition of this book and on our web page, as well as recommend your institution to prospective/current students. We could also collaborate on developing improvement plans for our campus.

To those institutions that continue to violate the civil and consumer rights of female students, we will publicize your unwillingness to engage in effective prevention efforts and recommend that prospective/current students enroll elsewhere. We will also work to deny accreditation and funding to any school that fails to effectively protect student civil rights.

The final decision is up to each institution. We would much rather work together to rid higher education of the scourge of faculty sexual harassment. However, we won't shy away from an adversarial relationship if all else fails.

Conclusions

We hope that the information in this chapter will help you evaluate how well your current or prospective university protects student civil and consumer rights on campus. You deserve a school with a vigorous sexual harassment prevention program and an uncompromising commitment to protect your rights! If an institution fails to meet your expectations on this vital issue, exercise your power as a consumer and take your business and your tuition dollars someplace else! Good luck!

CHAPTER 6

Preparing Yourself to be "Harassment-Proof"

Elaine was a sophomore, majoring in engineering at an urban commuter campus. After class one evening, the professor asked her if she could come with him to his office to discuss a possible summer internship with a local manufacturer. Elaine was excited about the opportunity and followed the professor.

After entering the office, the professor offered Elaine a chair, closed the door, and then briefly described the internship. Within minutes, he abruptly changed the subject and began to talk about how beautiful and sexy he thought Elaine was.

She was beginning to feel very uneasy. The professor related that he was recently divorced and very lonely. He moved his chair closer to Elaine and placed his hand on her knee. She was now trembling with dread.

The professor told her that they were a perfect couple. He leaned in and gave her a quick kiss on the forehead and fondled her breast.

Elaine was absolutely terrified and stunned. She struggled to push him away and quickly ran out of the office.

Elaine, like most other women victimized by faculty sexual predators, was totally unprepared to deal effectively with the harasser and placed herself in a very compromising situation. The primary purpose of this chapter is to fully prepare you to confront sexual harassment if and when it occurs, while taking precautionary steps to minimize the probability that you will be victimized. Quite simply, the goal is to make you "harassment-proof"!

Our comprehensive preparation approach consists of three major components: knowledge, prevention, and response development. We will fully discuss each one below.

Knowledge

You've heard the old saying that "knowledge is power." This is certainly true when it comes to protecting yourself against faculty sexual predators.

Knowledge entails a thorough understanding of sexual harassment as it occurs in academic settings. Specifically, we feel that it is critical to be fully knowledgeable about: (a) the definition of sexual harassment, as well as concrete examples, (b) your specific legal and consumer rights, (c) how universities operate and their typical policies and procedures, (d) the common characteristics and techniques of faculty sexual predators, (e) the options you have for filing complaints, (f) complaint filing procedures, (g) strategies to collect objective evidence to document your complaint, and (h) how to protect yourself from being victimized.

We have attempted to comprehensively address all of these essential topics in this book. By being fully informed, we are confident that you will significantly reduce the likelihood of becoming a harassment victim.

Prevention

The second component of an effective preparation program involves taking precautionary steps to prevent the problem from occurring in the first place. We offer the following specific recommendations.

First, try to enroll at a university that is committed to protecting your civil and consumer rights. Chapter 5 provides several suggestions for how to identify and evaluate an institution, along with information about selected universities that are already doing a reasonably good job.

Unfortunately, the majority of universities are not serious about protecting your civil and consumer rights. Our firm conviction is that you should spend your hard-earned tuition dollars only at institutions that are aggressively committed to guaranteeing that your civil and consumer rights are not violated. Don't enroll at a school that treats you otherwise!

A second preventive measure involves using a form that we developed for use with individual faculty members before you enroll in their classes (see

Figure 6-1). It simply asks them to verify that they do not have a prior disciplinary record for sexual harassment/sexual misconduct involving students.

Figure 6-1

College Student Consumer Rights Request Form
Concerning Faculty Sexual Harassment/Sexual Misconduct

To: (faculty name and address)   _____

                                         _____

                                         _____

From: (student name and address)   _____

                                         _____

                                         _____

As a student consumer of higher education, I have a right to know, before enrolling in a college course, whether the professor teaching the class has a prior disciplinary record for sexual harassment and/or sexual misconduct involving students.

I am considering enrollment in one of your classes, please assist me in exercising my right as a consumer by indicating below whether you have a prior disciplinary record for sexual harassment and/or sexual misconduct involving students.

Please **complete** this form, **sign** it, **date** it, and **mail** it to me at the address listed above. Thank you in advance for your cooperation.

Do you,_____
                 (printed faculty name)

have a prior disciplinary record for sexual harassment and/or sexual misconduct involving students (please check one)?

                                    _____Yes

                                    _____No

_____   _____

(faculty signature)   (date)

Who in their right mind would take a class from a professor with a past record of abusing students? We feel that every student has the consumer right to know about this critically important information that is essential in making sound enrollment decisions.

Ideally, completed and signed forms for all university faculty should be available for your review, prior to completing your class schedule. If the institution refuses to collect and compile this data, the student government or newspaper could assume this collective responsibility. If not available on your campus, you or your parent should deliver a form to each professor on your tentative schedule and ask that it be completed and returned to you prior to registration.

Don't be surprised if the response from many faculty members is less than positive. We have identified three major reasons why most professors refuse to complete and sign the form. First, they may have a prior disciplinary record for sexual harassment/sexual misconduct involving students. Second, they may be supportive of their harassing colleagues and part of the "good-old-boys-network". Third, they may simply not respect your rights as a consumer and be outraged that you dare to question them in this manner.

Regardless of the reasons for failing to complete the form, we strongly recommend that you avoid taking classes from any professor who so clearly disregards your consumer and/or civil rights. There are decent, honorable, competent, student-oriented professors at all universities. Your task is to identify them and take their classes!

Our third preventive measure entails a set of simple rules that you should always follow when interacting with university professors. They are designed to "short circuit" the harassment process and stop it before it starts.

Rule #1: Never go to a professor's office by yourself! Always take a friend along. If the professor wishes to speak to you privately, your friend can wait outside his office. Once inside, insist that the office door remain open by saying something like, "I would be more comfortable if we could keep the door open" or "I would prefer that the door remain open". Good professors will graciously honor your request, while harassers will be thwarted by the nearby presence of your friend. Most faculty sexual predators prefer to operate in private and behind closed doors. By refusing to interact with them in such settings, you can successfully stop any harassment before it begins.

Rule #2: Never agree to meet a professor at his home/apartment, a bar/restaurant, a park or isolated area, or more obviously a motel/hotel. If a professor needs to talk to you about an academic matter, he should do it before/after class or in his university office. Once again, it is essential to refuse a professor's request to meet at any location that would be conducive to attempted harassment.

Rule #3: When on field trips or class outings, refuse to be alone with the professor and always stay in the presence of other students. Remember, harassers like to operate by isolating their target victim and then beginning their sexual advances. Don't give them the chance.

Rule #4: Never consume alcohol and become intoxicated in the presence of a professor. Women students who drink to excess in situations, in which a harasser is present, significantly increase their probability of being victimized. When one's judgment is substantially clouded by alcohol, one's vulnerability to faculty sexual predators rises dramatically. Never allow yourself to be in such a situation. This same advice also certainly applies to drug use.

Consistently following the above four simple rules will effectively rob harassers of the settings in which they prefer to operate. Don't allow the enemy to engage you on turf of his own choice and you can make yourself virtually harassment-proof!

Response Development

The third and final component of our recommended preparation program involves formulating and practicing an effective STOP-RESPONSE! to sexual harassment if and when it occurs. Your STOP-RESPONSE! should be initiated at the first indication that harassment is beginning.

Let's be crystal clear about what should trigger an immediate STOP-RESPONSE! It is never appropriate for a professor with academic responsibility for you as a student to initiate sexually explicit comments, sexual advances, sexual contact, or other sexually oriented behaviors! Never! Under no circumstances! If you encounter such conduct on the part of a professor, you should automatically and emphatically implement your STOP-RESPONSE!

Elements of an effective STOP-RESPONSE! include the following. First, try to overcome your natural feelings of anger, fear, or disgust and remain calm. We know this is easier said than done, but it is essential to keep a calm clear mind throughout an episode like this. Taking slow deep breaths can be helpful in keeping you at your baseline. Practice is also invaluable, as we will discuss below.

Second, look the harasser squarely in the eyes! Sustained, stern eye contact dramatically communicates two powerful messages. Number 1—you are not scared or intimidated and Number 2—you are dead serious about your message.

Third, use a firm, assertive tone of voice when responding. This also conveys self-confidence and lack of fear.

Fourth, choose a verbal statement to unambiguously communicate that the professor's comment/behavior was unwelcome and offensive. Some examples include:

- "I don't appreciate what you just said (or did), and would like you to stop!"
- "The comment you just made is offensive to me (or makes me very uncomfortable), and I want you to stop!"
- "What you just said (or did) makes me very uneasy, and I want you to stop!"

Fifth, if the harassment involves an attempted sexual assault, respond aggressively to end it! Although only a very small percentage of academic sexual harassment involves sexual assault, you need to be fully prepared to decisively deal with it. We recommend taking a self-defense course for women or martial arts class to develop proficiency and confidence in protecting yourself. This is an important life-skill for everyone to have.

You may also consider purchasing and carrying teargas spray, pepper spray, or a small stun gun. These devices can instantly disable even the most aggressive attacker. Make sure you know how to safely and effectively operate whatever protective device you choose to carry. Also, confirm that it is legal in your state.

Comfort Level and Practice

It is critical that you are comfortable with whatever STOP-RESPONSE! you formulate. Trying to do or say something that doesn't fit your personality usually won't work in the long run. This may require some experimentation on your part until you find the "right" combination of verbal and nonverbal behaviors for you.

It is also essential that you practice your STOP-RESPONSE! This can be done by role-playing with your counselor, advisor, supportive professors, friends, family members, or classmates. If nothing else, practice in front of a mirror. Repeated practice will help you "overlearn" your STOP-RESPONSE! and enhance your ability to successfully deliver it in a stressful situation.

Written STOP-RESPONSE!

If you are reluctant, uncomfortable, or unable to verbally confront your harasser, you may consider writing him a brief note. You should clearly identify the specific behaviors that are objectionable and offensive to you. Also, be sure to communicate the unwelcome nature of those behaviors and that you would like them to stop. Lastly, be sure to keep a copy of the letter for your files.

Predator Reaction.

Most faculty sexual predators will be stunned by an effective STOP-RESPONSE! Remember, they prey on those who are vulnerable, passive, and weak. A boldly implemented STOP-RESPONSE! screams that you are anything but vulnerable, passive, or weak! Harassers are basically cowards who only engage those who are less powerful than themselves and will typically retreat quickly and try to suggest that they were "only joking" or "didn't mean anything by it". Some might even apologize and then swiftly move on in search of another potential victim.

In extremely isolated instances, faculty sexual predators will continue their harassment after a strong STOP-RESPONSE!, seeing you as a challenge. You should then aggressively collect evidence to document their behavior (see Chapter 8) and file a formal complaint (see Chapter 7).

Conclusions

You need to be well informed, strong, resolute, and aggressive in preparing yourself to deal with faculty sexual predators. If you fully implement the recommendations made in this chapter, we are highly confident that you will become virtually "harassment-proof" and never bear the agony of being victimized!

CHAPTER 7

Filing a Complaint

Forty-five students attending a sexual harassment prevention seminar were asked the following question by the facilitator:

How many of you know how or where to file a complaint involving sexual harassment? No one raised his or her hand.

This disturbing lack of student awareness unfortunately characterizes many universities today and serves as a powerful deterrent to filing complaints. In fact, research indicates that only 2% to 3% of women who are sexually harassed in higher education actually file a formal complaint. Unfortunately, institutions seem quite content to keep students uninformed. From their viewpoint, fewer complaints mean fewer problems to deal with.

Our objectives in this chapter are to introduce the various options that students have to file complaints, how these complaints are typically processed, and the pros and cons of each approach. We hope to demystify and simplify the challenge facing any student victim of sexual harassment who wishes to file a complaint.

Prerequisites for Filing a Complaint

Courage

Filing a complaint of sexual harassment against a university professor requires an extraordinary amount of courage. The process is replete with a variety of potentially serious academic and personal risks. For example, the offending professor and his "colleagues" can retaliate against you with lower or failing grades, disapproval of your thesis or dissertation topic, revocation of financial aid or scholarships, and negative references to potential employers or graduate schools. Some unscrupulous professors have used personal threats, stalking, and other forms of intimidation to persuade students to drop their complaint. If you file a lawsuit against a professor and/or institution, you can also expect to be ruthlessly questioned by their attorneys. The professor will be portrayed as the helpless victim, with you as a scheming, promiscuous tramp.

All of this can cause a great deal of stress and apprehension. If prolonged and serious enough, physical and psychological problems can develop.

Faculty sexual predators rely on these potent potential consequences to discourage their victims from filing a complaint. However, if no one ever filed a complaint, the harassing behaviors would continue unabated. Faculty harassers would never be reported and never disciplined for violating student civil rights.

Thus, it is imperative that anyone who feels they have been sexually harassed should file a formal complaint, using one of the options discussed in this chapter. It is critical that you demonstrate the personal courage needed to defend your civil rights and those of other women.

We commend and admire those who have evidenced this remarkable courage by formally filing sexual harassment complaints. Your stories need to be widely shared and used to inspire others.

Perseverance

Resolving complaints of academic sexual harassment/sexual misconduct can take anywhere from several months to years, if a case goes to court. Universities have a vested interest in extending this process as long as possible. Their unstated hope is that the student victim graduates, transfers to another school, drops out altogether, or becomes so frustrated with the protracted proceedings that the complaint is dropped.

When you file a sexual harassment complaint, you need to be prepared for a long, drawn-out process. This requires a great deal of perseverance and resolve. Since timely resolution or closure occurs rarely, you will be forced to deal with all of the potential stresses mentioned above for an extended time frame. Success depends upon your ability to maintain commitment and intensity in the face of protracted uncertainty. This is a test that few people can pass alone— thus, leading to our third prerequisite to complaint filing.

Social and Emotional Support

We have consistently found that those women who do file complaints of academic sexual harassment rely on solid social support networks for encouragement, strength, empathy, and motivation. These support networks can consist of family members, close friends, counselors/therapists, or concerned professors/administrators.

Ready access to an emotionally supportive social network can help you in several ways by:

- providing validation of your assessment of the situation in which the harassment occurred and your decision to file a complaint,
- fueling your courage to file a complaint,
- accompanying you during the filing process and throughout any interviews or hearings that take place,
- assisting you in dealing with the inevitable stress that arises and locating professional therapists, if needed, and
- maintaining your commitment and resolve during the process.

Clearly you can see the important ways in which a support network can help a courageous victim of sexual harassment file a formal complaint. If you have been victimized, make sure you have an active, energetic, compassionate network to help support you.

Evidence

Before you file a complaint of sexual harassment/sexual misconduct against a professor and/or university, it is absolutely essential that you have solid evidence to corroborate your charges. (The topic of collecting evidence is fully discussed in the next chapter.) Without convincing evidence, your complaint has little chance of being successful.

Evidence to support your claims should be completely assembled before filing your complaint. The reason is fairly clear. Once a complaint has been filed and the alleged offender notified, the harassing actions are likely to stop immediately and your opportunities to collect evidence will dramatically diminish.

If your case is based solely on your word versus the professor's, your chances of success are remote—not impossible, but highly unlikely. Thus, a solid evidence collection strategy must be formulated and implemented before you file your complaint.

Complaint Filing Options

As a victim of faculty sexual harassment, you have a number of different complaint filing alternatives. The correct choice depends upon the specific characteristics of your situation. We will try to provide you with the information necessary to make this important decision.

There are seven primary complaint filing options. They include: university, local law enforcement authorities, Office for Civil Rights (OCR)-Direct, OCR-Delayed, OCR-Advocate, civil court, and the media. We will discuss each of them and provide the following information: (a) appropriate use guidelines, (b) how to file a complaint, and (c) major pros and cons. In the first section, we will devote more attention to our discussion of the university complaint filing process so that you will better understand why other options typically offer higher probabilities of success.

University Complaint

Universities process sexual harassment complaints in a variety of ways. However, there are certain basic steps that most institutions follow. They typically include the three discussed below.

Steps Involved

Step One—Affirmative Action/Equal Employment Opportunity Officer. Complaints are typically filed with a campus Affirmative Action Officer or Equal Employment Opportunity Officer. This person and her/his staff are then responsible for conducting an initial investigation of the allegations. Involved parties and any witnesses are interviewed, evidence is reviewed, and a final report of findings is usually prepared.

Step Two—Faculty Hearing or Review Board. The preliminary report of findings is commonly submitted to a hearing board or review committee. This group typically consists exclusively or predominantly of faculty members elected by their peers to serve. At some institutions, a token administrator and/or student may be included.

The faculty board begins by reviewing the preliminary report of findings and evidence collected in the case. They typically have the option of interviewing the student complainant, accused faculty member, and any potential witnesses. Once their deliberations are completed, a final report of findings and recommendations is submitted to the senior campus administrator. This report includes any recommended disciplinary action for the professor.

Step Three—Senior Administrator. Upon receiving the faculty board's report of findings and recommendations, a senior university administrator (president, provost, chancellor) typically makes the final decision concerning complaint resolution. This includes a determination of: (1) whether the alleged harassment occurred or not, (2) any corrective or compensatory action needed to address the student victim's concerns, and (3) any disciplinary action to be taken against the faculty member.

Obstacles

The complaint process described above presents a number of staggering and often hidden obstacles to any student who attempts to use it. In fact, these obstacles are so powerful that the overwhelming majority of female students who have been sexually harassed do not file a complaint with the university. As mentioned earlier, research findings indicate that only 2% to 3% of student victims actually file a formal complaint with the school. Unfortunately, the percentage of women who are ultimately successful is pitifully small!

There is a powerful message in these statistics. Something is seriously wrong with the complaint processing system. It is certainly not "student-friendly" and acts to discourage anyone from coming forward.

Major problems with the steps typically involved in the way universities process student complaints include the following.

Problems with Campus Affirmative Action or EEO Officer Investigations

- the Affirmative Action Officer and her/his staff are all employees of the university.

- the Affirmative Action Officer and her/his staff have a vested interest in protecting the university and its faculty at the expense of students.
- the Affirmative Action Officer often knows the alleged harasser and has had collegial interaction with him in the past.
- the Affirmative Action Officer has often had little or no formal professional training in properly conducting investigations and collecting evidence.
- the Affirmative Action Officer has no professional or legal responsibility (as do sworn police officers) to report potential criminal violations to appropriate law enforcement authorities; thus, cases involving sexual assault are handled internally rather than properly involving the police.
- the Affirmative Action Officer typically has a staff and budget that are insufficient to conduct timely, thorough, professionally sound investigations.
- the Affirmative Action Officer is typically unwilling to contact other students who are likely to have been harassed by the same professor; preferring instead to believe that unless a student comes forward, there is no reason to initiate contact.
- in "he said, she said" cases, the Affirmative Action Officer is often easily persuaded by the articulate arguments of the faculty harasser that commonly include:

  - "the student misunderstood what I said or did"
  - "the student struggles academically and was either trying to persuade me to give her a better grade or trying to retaliate against me for giving her a bad grade"
  - "the complaint is obviously a false one, as the only evidence is her own testimony"
  - "I have the academic freedom to say and do whatever I want to in my class"
  - "there was an important educational reason for what I said or did"
  - "my constitutionally guaranteed right of free speech permits me to say anything I want"

Under these circumstances, a truly independent, unbiased, and objective investigation is virtually <u>impossible</u>.

<u>Note: False Complaints</u>. Researchers have estimated that false complaints against professors comprise less than 1% of the total number filed. Remember that only 2% to 3% of women who have been harassed actually file a formal complaint. Although false complaints are occasionally filed, the frequency is truly microscopic— .02% to .03%.

As you might suspect, university administrators and faculty grossly overestimate this percentage and exaggerate the likelihood that students, disgruntled over poor grades, would file harassment complaints. This is often an argument used in opposition to offering student training/education on sexual harassment or conducting a sexual harassment survey on campus. The plain truth is, female students are very very unlikely to file deliberately false complaints!

<u>Problems with Faculty Boards</u>

- membership on review boards is typically restricted to professors from the campus, without any representation from students, parents, the community, or faculty from other universities;
- members of the faculty review board are all university employees;
- review board members commonly have a strong vested interest in protecting faculty members first, the university second, and students a distant third;
- review board members are often elected by campus professors or appointed by faculty leaders based upon how vigorously they defend faculty rights; the mindset or sentiment involves an unquestioning commitment to "protect our own" against attacks from everyone else;
- review board members often have the attitude that "I'll scratch your back now, if you scratch mine later"; in other words, I will blindly defend you against the student's complaints today, if you will do the same for me in the future;
- in many instances, review board members have known and worked with the alleged harasser for years; they may even be friends or tennis partners;

- review board members are readily persuaded by the articulate points often made by faculty harassers, suggesting that they are really the victims in the complaint process;
- in some situations, elected or appointed review board members are themselves sexual harassers and have unpublicized histories of violating student civil rights;
- given the high percentage of male faculty at U.S. universities (65%), review board members are more likely to be males, resulting in the following kinds of problems:

  - a tendency to devalue and disrespect women;
  - a generally unsympathetic orientation toward female students filing complaints;
  - a feeling that sexual harassment is only a "woman's issue" and a product of radical feminists;
  - a belief that sexual access to women students is a "perk" of the job;
  - a belief that sexual conquests of women students are a sign of virility and masculinity;
  - a strong commitment to the "good-old-boys-network";
  - a sense that "boys will be boys" when presented with attractive young women;
  - a "knee-jerk" reaction that all complaints are false and related to receiving poor grades;

- review board members often fear that a negative decision against the harasser could lead to some form of retaliation against them in the future; if the harasser happens to be a member of various faculty committees that make decisions about raises, promotions, tenure, travel funds, and/or sabbaticals, board members may be especially reluctant to vote against him;
- review board members typically have little or no professional training in conducting investigations, reviewing evidence, or interviewing witnesses; they also have limited knowledge about sexual harassment laws, regulations, and case rulings;
- given these major characteristics of faculty review boards, students are <u>unlikely</u> to receive a fair, objective, unbiased evaluation of their complaints;

- for the reasons mentioned above, review boards are typically unwilling to recommend anything but the most mild punishments for faculty offenders; at best, recommended sanctions represent a "slap on the wrist"; at worst, they can actually reward perpetrators (at one university, the "punishment" recommended by a faculty review board for a professor who confessed to having sex with a teenage student was a one-semester suspension from teaching duties—at full pay!).

Problems with Senior University Administrators

- senior administrators are all employees of the university.
- senior administrators are motivated to protect the interests of the university first and foremost, followed by the faculty.
- senior administrators typically have had little or no professional training in conducting investigations, reviewing evidence, or sexual harassment enforcement regulations and case law.
- in some instances, senior administrators are themselves sexual harassers (at one university, the top administrator was forced to resign from his position after several women students, faculty, and staff filed formal complaints about his sexual harassment that had been occurring for years!).
- senior administrators are often extremely reluctant to take disciplinary action against any professor for fear of antagonizing the entire faculty.
- senior administrators are often fearful that faculty harassers will initiate lawsuits against the university if they are disciplined in any way as a result of a sexual harassment investigation.
- with very few exceptions, senior university administrators are not known for their bold, decisive leadership; instead they are often selected and retained on the basis of their deferential attitude toward faculty and lack of strong leadership skills.
- there is typically no oversight, external review, or public review of administrative decisions in sexual harassment cases; thus, administrators are free to quickly and quietly resolve cases in the best interests of the university and faculty, while ignoring student civil rights.

- the overwhelming majority of senior university administrators in the U.S. are men; thus, the male biases and attitudes discussed in the preceding section are even more problematic when they apply to the final decision maker.
- once more, the nature of the university complaint processing system involving senior academic administrators insures that student complaints will not be handled objectively or fairly.

Pros and Cons of Filing a University Complaint

Filing a sexual harassment complaint directly with a university has little to recommend it, other than meeting the Supreme Court requirement to formally notify the institution and provide an opportunity for corrective action. We noted in Chapter 3 that as long as the university takes some type of action and is not "deliberately indifferent" to the student's complaint, the institution cannot be held legally responsible for any damage done by the harasser. Thus, don't be surprised if there is a minimal response from the university, aiming only to avoid legal liability and preserve faculty privileges and rights.

There are several substantial disadvantages associated with filing a university complaint. First, there is a pervasive, strong pro-faculty bias throughout the system. Second, the investigation will often be conducted in an unprofessional, biased, and excessively time-consuming manner.

Third, there is little likelihood that the offending professor will receive any significant punishment. In fact, he may even be "rewarded" with a suspension of teaching responsibilities for a given semester at full pay—essentially a 3 to 4 month paid vacation!

Fourth, there is essentially no chance that you will receive any significant compensation from the university for your suffering as a victim. Fifth, the university is unlikely to initiate any substantive improvements in prevention or education programs as a result of your complaint. Since sexual harassment incidence statistics are not publicly reported, many members of the university community are never informed about the horrible cases that occur and thus see no justification for reform efforts.

Finally, when you file a complaint, there is always a risk that the harasser, his supporters, or the institution may retaliate against you. The retaliation could be academic or personal in nature. For instance, you may receive unwarranted bad grades, fail to be considered for scholarships or special programs, or get poor letters of recommendation for work or graduate school.

Any type of retaliation for filing a complaint represents an additional violation of your civil rights and should be carefully documented (see the next chapter on collecting evidence). When confronted with retaliatory actions, we strongly recommend that you: (a) contact an attorney to represent you and provide advice about protecting yourself and (b) seriously consider taking your complaint to an external agency—the Office for Civil Rights of the Department of Education, the local police, or civil court.

Retaliation adds further insult to your initial injury as a victim of sexual harassment. It demonstrates utter contempt for your civil rights and should be aggressively addressed. This will require a great deal of courage and tenacity on your part. Try to find strength and encouragement from your support group.

Note. Many students incorrectly assume that writing comments about a professor's harassing conduct on course evaluations at the end of the semester constitutes filing a written complaint and leads to an investigation. Most institutions do not consider such remarks as complaints (even if signed) and do not initiate any investigation into the allegations.

We know many students who were very disappointed to learn that the university would not investigate comments on course evaluations. In order to initiate a formal investigation, virtually all universities require a signed, written statement of allegations from the student victim.

Local Law Enforcement Authorities Complaint

If you feel that a professor's harassing behaviors might involve violations of criminal law, a complaint is best filed directly with local law enforcement authorities; for example, city, county, or state police. We have provided a list and simple description of potential criminal charges associated with sexual harassment cases in Table 7-1.

Table 7-1

Potential Criminal Offenses Associated with Sexual Harassment Cases[1]

Criminal Offense	General Definition[2]
Rape	Forcing or threatening a person to engage in sexual intercourse.
Sexual Assault	Forcing or threatening a person to engage in a sex act.
Sexual Contact	Intentional touching or contact with the intimate parts of another person's body for the purpose of sexual gratification for the actor or humiliation/degradation of the victim.
Assault	A threat or attempt to forcefully inflict bodily harm on a victim, creating the apprehension that injury is imminent.
Battery	The use of physical force to inflict bodily harm on a victim.
Stalking	Repeatedly following a person in such a way as to alarm the victim and instill fear of harm.
Cyberstalking	Repeated use of the Internet or e-mail to threaten, harass, or embarrass the victim.

[1]Adapted from Random House Webster's Dictionary of the Law (2000) by J. E. Clapp and Barron's Law Dictionary (1996) by S.H. Gifis.

[2]Specific definitions vary from state to state. Contact an attorney or consult relevant statutes to determine the definition that applies in your state.

In general, criminal laws are violated if the harassment involves coerced sexual activity, forced physical or sexual contact, physical or sexual threats, physical injury, involuntary confinement, or stalking. If any of these or similar behaviors are involved, you should definitely file a complaint directly with law enforcement officials. Specific questions about whether a criminal violation has occurred should be directed to a local police department, prosecutor's office, or experienced attorney.

Filing a complaint typically entails completing a detailed incidence report describing what happened. Police officers will then conduct an investigation. Based upon the results of their investigation and the severity of the alleged offense, local prosecutors may elect to file formal criminal charges against the professor, seek a warrant for his arrest, and arrange to schedule a trial.

All of this can sound quite intimidating, and it is! We strongly recommend that you call upon someone in your support network to accompany you during the complaint filing process. Also, a sympathetic, knowledgeable lawyer can be invaluable in helping you navigate through the complex criminal justice system. Trusted sources for attorney referrals include: (a) the National Organization for Women (NOW) Legal Defense and Education Fund—www.nowldef.org and (b) the American Association of University Women (AAUW) Legal Advocacy Fund—www.aauw.org.

Note: Don't File Potential Criminal Complaints With Your University. Several years ago a retired university police chief emphatically asserted that when possible criminal violations are involved in a sexual harassment episode, a student should immediately bypass the university complaint processing procedure and go directly to the local police. He substantiated his assertion with the following observations.

First, as mentioned earlier in this chapter, university affirmative action officers designated to receive initial complaints of sexual harassment are not legally required to submit suspected criminal violations to local law enforcement authorities and are typically not trained or qualified to make informed decisions about criminal law violations. The retired police chief contended that often, academic sexual harassment cases, with likely criminal violations, were never properly referred to the appropriate authorities for prosecution.

Second, the retired chief noted that many university police departments were in fact staffed with security guards, as opposed to sworn police offices. Security guards do not have the legal obligation to report suspected criminal violations to local prosecutors, as do sworn police officers. Thus, you cannot assume that evidence of criminal violations will be submitted to the appropriate prosecutor's office if your complaint was filed with campus security guards. In order to avoid this situation, the retired chief again recommended going directly to local police.

Finally, the chief noted that because criminal charges against a faculty member can be devastating to an institution's image and enrollment, senior administrators at times exert tremendous pressure on university police departments to placate the victim and handle the case internally. Unfortunately, appropriate criminal charges are then not filed.

For these very powerful reasons, the retired university police chief strongly recommended that in cases involving potential criminal violations, victims file complaints directly with local law enforcement authorities. We wholeheartedly concur with his advice.

Pros and Cons of Filing a Complaint with Law Enforcement Authorities

Filing a complaint with local law enforcement officials has the following four principal advantages. First and foremost, you will benefit from a professional, relatively unbiased, and timelier investigation into the alleged criminal violations. Second, a determination of guilt or innocence will be made by individuals (judge or jury) who are independent and not formally associated with the university. Third, if the professor is found guilty of criminal conduct, the punishment will be appropriately commensurate with the severity of the offense and could involve a long jail term. Fourth, if a professor is convicted in a high-profile criminal case involving a student, there is a significant likelihood that the university will be pressured to implement meaningful campus reforms.

There are at least seven potential drawbacks of filing your complaint with law enforcement officials. First, there has been a longstanding anti-female bias in the criminal justice system when sex-related charges are filed. This is most dramatically evidenced in the way many rape victims are treated as if they were responsible for the attack. Although we feel that this anti-female bias is weakening in the United States, you should be prepared to deal with it when it occurs. A supportive attorney can be very helpful in determining the most appropriate response.

A second disadvantage involves the slow case processing that characterizes many criminal courts. A trial and final verdict can easily take several months or even years in some instances.

Third, you will incur potentially substantial legal fees in securing a competent attorney to represent your interests. Fourth, when depositions are taken and during the trial, you can expect to be bombarded with insulting, demeaning, and offensive questions by the university's and/or professor's attorney, as he/she tries to demonstrate that you were responsible for what happened or willingly complied.

A fifth disadvantage entails the potential stress and embarrassment associated with media coverage of a high-profile case involving criminal charges against a professor. Sixth, there is no likelihood that you will receive compensation as the victim of the crime(s). Finally, the seventh disadvantage is the ever-present possibility that the harassers, his supporters, or university supporters who resent the adverse media attention may retaliate against you academically or personally.

Office for Civil Rights (OCR)—Direct Complaint

As discussed in Chapter 3, the Office for Civil Rights (OCR) within the U.S. Department of Education was established in 1972 as the primary enforcement agency for sexual harassment in academic settings. Complaints may be submitted directly to the appropriate regional OCR office (see Appendix A for a list of the national and ten regional offices and their addresses). Students are not required to file their complaint with the institution first.

This filing option is recommended for use when the following conditions exist. First, a professor sexually harassed you within the last 180 days as required by OCR regulations. Second, you are confident that no criminal violations occurred. Third, you do not trust the university to stop the harassment, properly conduct a professional, unbiased investigation, or appropriately punish the offender. This judgment could be based upon information about how such complaints have been handled in the past.

If these criteria apply to your case, we recommend that you strongly consider filing your complaint directly with the OCR. It is unfortunate but true that most universities do not ever inform students of their right to this filing option. Obviously, they clearly prefer to handle complaints internally.

Equally unfortunate is the OCR's inability to effectively publicize the availability of this and other filing options for students. The problem is ostensibly a function of inadequate funding. We suspect, however, that universities have had a role in insuring that students are not informed of their filing rights with the OCR.

A complaint is initiated with the OCR by completing and submitting a detailed Discrimination Complaint Form. This document is available from any of the ten regional offices. A copy is provided in Appendix C.

Once a direct complaint has been received, the OCR will formally contact the university and inform appropriate officials of the allegations. The institution is then provided an opportunity to investigate the complaint and initiate necessary corrective and disciplinary actions.

A written summary of the university's response to the complaint is then supplied to the OCR. A trained professional OCR investigator will carefully review the university's response and issue a final report of findings and recommendations. Copies are sent to the complainant, the alleged harasser, and the institution.

Unfortunately, the institution is not required to follow any of the recommendations contained in the report and the OCR is essentially powerless to force compliance. Its only official power, reserved for the most serious cases of university misconduct, involves recommending that federal funding support to the institution be terminated. As pointed out by the American Association of University Women Legal Advocacy Fund in A License for Bias: Sex Discrimination, Schools, and Title IX (2000), the OCR has "never [emphasis added] exercised its authority to withhold federal funds from an offending institution." Absent more effective tools to mandate university compliance with report recommendations, the OCR is reduced to a "toothless tiger". In contrast, the OCR's sister organization in the area of workplace sexual harassment (the EEOC, Equal Employment Opportunity Commission) has the power, authority, and funding to sue employers in federal court to force compliance with recommended remedies.

Pros and Cons of Filing an OCR-Direct Complaint

There are four major advantages of filing your complaint directly with the OCR. First, since filing a complaint with the OCR triggers notification of your allegations to the university, you meet the Supreme Court's requirement to formally notify the institution of the harassment. Second, you can expect a professional, unbiased review of the university's investigation of your complaint. Third, an independent decision about the harasser's guilt or innocence will be made by a trained professional who is not associated with the university, after reviewing the institution's report. Fourth, even though the OCR is relatively powerless, the perceived significance associated with a federal agency's final report serves to encourage some institutions to initiate stronger campus prevention and education programs.

There are several disadvantages associated with an OCR-direct complaint. First, due to limited staffing and resources, case processing is very slow—often taking several months or longer. Second, for reasons mentioned above, neither the institution nor professor will likely face serious punishment. Third, you will not likely receive any compensation as a victim of sexual harassment. Fourth, as is always true, once a complaint is filed, you face potential retaliation from the harasser, his supporters, and even the institution.

Office for Civil Rights (OCR)-Delayed Complaint

If you have already filed a formal sexual harassment complaint with your university, the OCR will not allow you to file a direct complaint with them. Instead, they require you to wait until the institution has completed its investigation, issued a final report, and taken appropriate corrective action.

At that point, if you are displeased in any way with the university's final report or actions taken, you may file a complaint with the OCR, asking them to review your case. It is important that this paperwork be filed within 60 days of the date that the institution's final report was issued.

The form used is the same one that is completed when filing a direct complaint and is contained in Appendix C. In addition, you must attach a copy of the university's final report.

Pros and Cons of Filing an OCR-Delayed Complaint

The advantages and disadvantages associated with the OCR-Delayed complaint are similar to those for the OCR-Direct complaint. The only difference is the timing of the OCR's involvement in the case and assistance to you as the complainant.

Office for Civil Rights (OCR)—Advocate Complaint

Perhaps one of the most significant features of OCR guidelines on dealing with sexual harassment is the provision that allows concerned, sympathetic professors or administrators to file a complaint on your behalf. Thus, your advocate can file either an OCR-Direct or OCR-Delayed complaint for you, and the same statute of limitations/filing deadlines apply.

Your role in this process is three-fold. First, you must provide a signed statement of specific allegations against a faculty member. A copy of this must be attached to the complaint. Second, you must consent to have your advocate file the complaint. Third, you must agree to cooperate with the OCR in their review of the university's investigation and response to your complaint.

Pros and Cons of Filing an OCR-Advocate Complaint

Allowing an advocate to file a complaint on your behalf has similar advantages and disadvantages to personally filing your complaint, with three significant additional benefits. First, when an advocate files for you, it further legitimizes your complaint and the gravity of your allegations. In other words, there is more than one person who believes that a civil rights violation has occurred! Second, the advocate can serve to deflect criticism and retaliation away from you for filing the complaint. Instead, the advocate becomes the "lightening rod" and can focus any negative attention on himself/herself. Third, having someone who is willing to fight for you and with you makes the overall experience less threatening and stressful!

Civil Lawsuit Complaint

There are a wide variety of state and federal laws that can be used to initiate a civil lawsuit against individual harassers and/or universities for depriving you of your civil or consumer rights. Before pursuing this complaint option, it is imperative that you seek the advice of a competent, experienced, supportive attorney. To assist you in this process, we strongly recommend that you first contact the American Association of University Women Legal Advocacy Fund—www.aauw.org. This is an outstanding, nonprofit organization that provides funding, support, and attorney referrals to women pursuing legal action for sex discrimination (including sexual harassment) in higher education.

You should consider filing a civil lawsuit after any of the following have occurred and you believe that you were not compensated properly for the damage you suffered and/or the harasser and institution were not appropriately disciplined: (a) the university has completed its investigation of your complaint and issued its final report, (b) the OCR has issued a final report on its investigation of your direct, delayed, or advocate complaint, or (c) a verdict has been reached in a criminal trial against a faculty sexual predator and sentence imposed, if found guilty. In each of the above instances, if you feel that you have not been "made whole again" after suffering from the harasser's attack or that the perpetrator and his colluding institution have not been justly disciplined, you should seek the advice of a good attorney and consider filing a lawsuit.

If an attorney accepts your case, she/he will recommend the best way to file your complaint, that is, which state or federal statutes provide you with the highest probability of success. Once this decision has been made, a civil lawsuit is filed in either state or federal court.

After litigation has been initiated, it can take months or even years before your case is ever heard in court. Universities, of course, will typically engage in a variety of delaying tactics in the hope that you will become frustrated, graduate, or move away and ultimately drop the lawsuit. They will also typically try to intimidate you when your deposition is taken. The university attorney may ask you a set of insulting, demeaning questions designed to probe your morals, sexual behavior, and motives to entrap or seduce the "poor unsuspecting" professor.

The overwhelming majority of sexual harassment lawsuits are settled out-of-court, but only after the university has subjected you to a protracted, contentious pre-trial period. However, most institutions want to avoid the adverse publicity often associated with high-profile court cases. Use this knowledge to your advantage in pressing for a settlement.

Many attorneys will take your case on a contingency basis, meaning that their fee is contingent upon winning the case. Unfortunately, even in these instances, additional legal fees can quickly become burdensome, i.e., cost for an expert witness(es).

Pros and Cons of Filing a Civil Lawsuit

There are a number of potent advantages and disadvantages associated with filing a civil lawsuit against a harasser and his institution. Assuming you are able to locate a competent, supportive, aggressive attorney and you have strong evidence of wrongdoing, the following five beneficial outcomes can be achieved.

First, you will have a professional legal advocate for your civil and consumer rights, someone who will vigorously defend your interests. Second, if the case goes to trial, an independent, unbiased judge or jury with no connections to the institution will determine the guilt or innocence of the defendants.

Third, success in a civil trial provides you the opportunity to negatively impact the harasser and university by colleting punitive damages. Fourth, you also have the chance to be compensated for your pain, suffering, and other losses by receiving compensatory damages.

Fifth and finally, a high profile court case provides a powerful incentive to universities to initiate significant corrective action and reform. The adverse public opinion that such cases generate can often motivate otherwise unresponsive administrators to take academic sexual harassment complaints more seriously.

Offsetting these advantages is a set of six significant potential disadvantages that should be carefully considered before initiating a civil lawsuit. First, when suing an academic institution for sexual harassment, it can be challenging to prove that the university was "deliberately indifferent" to your complaint. This requirement originated as a result of a Supreme Court decision in 1998 and has made it much more difficult for victims to prevail against institutions.

We hope that intense lobbying efforts by several women's and civil rights groups will result in national legislation to correct this gross injustice to student victims of sexual harassment. Until such legislation is passed, we have four suggestions: (a) when there is evidence that the faculty sexual predator who victimized you has a prior record for harassing students, try to use this record to demonstrate that the university has been "deliberately indifferent" to his continuing violations of student civil rights and failed to take effective correction action, (b) ask your attorney to consider other federal or state statutes that could serve as the basis for your harassment claim, (c) consider using consumer fraud statutes to justify your complaint, and (d) target your lawsuit at the harasser only.

A second potential disadvantage of filing a civil lawsuit involves the typically slow processing of these cases through the courts—often taking several months or even years before a trial is conducted. Third, the expenses involved in hiring an attorney and pursuing your case can be substantial.

Fourth, you can expect opposing attorneys to grill you with insulting, demeaning, offensive questions during your deposition and at trial. Fifth, substantial stress, embarrassment, and loss of privacy are often unfortunate outcomes associated with litigation, especially if media attention is involved. Sixth, there is always the possibility that the harasser, his supporters, or the institution will retaliate against you academically or personally.

Media Complaint

Universities are notoriously slow in responding to any type of sexual harassment complaint. They often deliberately use strategies to prolong the investigation and delay a timely hearing or trial. The goal is to "drag out" the process and "wear you down." Their hope is that you will graduate, transfer to another school, dropout, or move away and lose interest in pursuing your complaint.

Institutions are also characteristically reluctant to effectively resolve harassment cases, compensate you in any way for your pain and suffering, or initiate necessary corrective actions. By "stonewalling" and refusing to budge, institutions hope to frustrate and demoralize you. Hopefully then, you would abandon your case.

One very powerful way to motivate institutions to quickly and satisfactorily resolve your complaint, as well as initiate corrective and preventive actions, is to threaten to "go to the press." If the threat is ignored, then contact local newspapers, magazines, radio stations, and/or television stations with your complaint. Unless there is a "sweetheart" relationship with the university, most media outlets would be keenly interested in a well-documented sexual harassment complaint that has not been promptly or effectively resolved by a university. If your case involves especially heinous conduct on the part of the harasser and an institution, you might even consider contacting national media outlets.

As a general rule, all universities are terrified of seriously adverse publicity that appears in the media. A story with lurid details about a faculty sexual predator and an institution's failure to appropriately respond can have an absolutely devastating impact on public relations, enrollment, and fund raising.

For example, one small regional university located in a rural area that was aggressively trying to expand its enrollment was simultaneously confronted with three sexual harassment complaints one summer. They all involved very serious civil rights violations. The young women and their families had hired attorneys and demanded and obtained a face-to-face meeting with the institution's senior administrator. At that meeting, the students insisted on a timely, thorough and complete investigation, prompt punishment of the offenders, compensation for their suffering, and mandatory training on preventing sexual harassment for all faculty and staff. If these demands were not met, the three threatened to go to the press with their stories and initiate civil lawsuits. The institution was given one month to meet the demands.

It is truly amazing how quickly and efficiently a university can function when self-preservation is the primary motive. Clearly understanding the gravity of the situation and the enormous risks involved, the administration was able to successfully meet every one of the students' demands within the allotted time. This included a substantial financial settlement for each of the three young women. We are convinced that this timely complaint resolution was only made possible by the credible threat of devastating media exposure.

Pros and Cons of Going to the Media with Your Complaint

The cost/benefit comparison associated with initiating a media complaint should be carefully considered. Potential advantages include: (a) quickly motivating the institution to take your case seriously and resolve it in a satisfactory manner, (b) quickly motivating the university to initiate significant reforms and preventive programs, (c) alerting other student victims to the common problem and encouraging them to file a complaint also, and (d) informing other students about the existence of the harassment problem on campus and hopefully helping them to avoid being victimized.

There are at least three potentially serious disadvantages when one goes public with a sexual harassment case. First, there may be a great deal of stress, embarrassment, and invasion of privacy that accompanies the media attention.

Second, there is the possibility of a lawsuit from the harasser for slander or defamation of character. For this reason, we strongly recommend seeking legal advice before going to the media.

Third, the threat of potential retaliation from the harasser, his supporters, or the institution should be considered. Negative media attention seems to intensify the motivation to retaliate, so be careful if you use this strategy.

Conclusions

Filing a sexual harassment complaint can be a frightening and intimidating prospect. Without question, there are substantial risks involved to you personally and academically. Many victims conclude that the anticipated costs far outweigh the "hoped-for" benefits. In fact, the overwhelming majority of female victims of sexual harassment do not file a formal complaint at all. They suffer in silence.

In spite of the risks, we encourage every victim to seriously consider filing an appropriate formal complaint. We hope the information in this chapter is helpful to you in deciding where and how to file your complaint.

Regardless of which option you choose, we strongly encourage you to seek active assistance from members of your social support network. A strong, empathetic, assertive supporter can be invaluable in helping you successfully pursue your complaint and deal more effectively with the inevitable obstacles that you will confront.

If no one ever filed a complaint against faculty sexual predators, the problem of sexual harassment on campus would continue unabated and probably increase in magnitude. Courageous women willing to come forward and file a complaint are absolutely essential to our collective efforts to attack this horrible problem. We admire their bravery and tenacity. We hope that you too can find the inspiration and resolve to fight for your civil rights and those of other collegiate women. We're on your side and will continue to work with you and others to eliminate sexual harassment at U.S. colleges and universities!

Final Note. If you were sexually harassed while performing work functions as a part-time or full-time university employee, you are covered by Title VII of the 1964 Civil Rights Act. The Equal Employment Opportunity Commission (EEOC) is the federal government agency charged with overseeing the enforcement of Title VII. For more detailed information about workplace sexual harassment, you can contact the EEOC directly at www.eeoc.gov or 1-800-669-4000 (TDD 1-800-669-6820).

CHAPTER 8

Collecting Evidence to Prove Your Case

Kristin found herself seated in a large conference room being questioned by a 5-member faculty committee. She had filed a sexual harassment complaint against one of her professors for propositioning her in his office as a way to improve her course grade from "C" to "A".

Many of the questions from the stern-faced committee were insulting and offensive:

"Is it safe to say that you are not a very serious student? Isn't it possible that you misunderstood what the professor was saying? Is your complaint a way to "get back at" the professor for giving you a "C" in the class? Did you go to the professor's office to proposition him in order to improve your course grade to an "A"?

Kristin's experience is all too common for female students filing a complaint of sexual harassment/sexual misconduct against a professor. It might seem like the "odds are against you" and they are! If your complaint is a case of "your word against his," 99.9% of the time, you will lose.

In this chapter, we will discuss the types of evidence needed when attempting to prove a sexual harassment complaint against a faculty member. We will then offer a number of specific recommendations about how to best collect the necessary evidence and dramatically improve your chances for success.

Evidence Collection Requirements

As a student filing a sexual harassment complaint against a university professor, it is critically important that you have detailed documentation and independent, objective supporting evidence. This is true regardless of whether your complaint is filed with the university, the Office for Civil Rights of the Department of Education, or federal/state courts.

Unfortunately, as we mentioned earlier, if it is your word versus the professor's, you have very little chance of prevailing. Success requires careful record keeping and assembling credible evidence to confirm your allegations. The better your documentation and the more evidence you have, the greater the likelihood of a successful resolution!

We realize that taking the steps to collect evidence against a professor can be time consuming, stressful, and even frightening. However, remember this— he has violated your civil rights. You do not deserve to be treated like this by anyone, much less a university professor whose salary you are helping to pay.

Now is the time to be bold, assertive, and self-confident. Build your case and then file your complaint, complete with supporting documentation and evidence! Good luck!

Warning: Be sure to keep the original copies of any documentation or evidence you collect for your files and potential use in future lawsuits. You can effectively file formal complaints with the university or OCR by including copies of your original documentation and evidence.

Evidence Collection Strategies

Below are seven specific suggestions about how to document what has happened to you and collect credible evidence to support your complaint.

1.   Incident Form. Keeping a written record of every sexual harassment incident is extremely important. Don't trust your memory; write down a description of the incident as soon as possible.

In Figure 8-1, we have provided a sample Sexual Harassment Incident Form for your use. It allows you to conveniently summarize important facts about the incident, including such things as date, time, place, other individuals present, what the harasser said or did, and how you responded. This type of information serves as excellent documentation when you file a complaint or go to court.

Figure 8-1

SEXUAL HARASSMENT INCIDENT FORM

DATE: _____

TIME INCIDENT OCCURRED: _____

PLACE INCIDENT OCCURRED: _____

NAMES OF OTHER PEOPLE PRESENT: _____

_____

_____

1.   Description of Sexual Harassment (What specifically did the professor say or do?)

_____

_____

_____

_____

_____

2.   In response to the Sexual Harassment, what did you say or do?

_____

_____

_____

_____

_____

3.   In response to the Sexual Harassment, how did you feel?

_____

_____

_____

_____

_____

4.   Did you take any action after the incident? If yes, what action(s)
        did you take?

        _____

        _____

        _____

        _____

        _____

5.   Did you talk with anyone after the incident? If yes, with whom
        did you talk and what was the content of your conversation?

        _____

        _____

        _____

        _____

        _____

2.   Witnesses. Individuals who were present when you were harassed can be an excellent source of supporting evidence concerning the harassing behaviors, if they are willing to cooperate and provide a signed statement about what happened. Witnesses can also be helpful in documenting your emotional state following the harassment. Their statements can provide invaluable evidence about how upset you were and what actions you took.

Unfortunately, many potential witnesses are often unwilling to get involved or take the risks associated with testifying against a professor. This can be especially discouraging when your classmates and "friends" refuse to cooperate and confirm the accuracy of your allegations.

Thus, don't rely solely on witnesses to support your complaint. They may or may not be willing to cooperate, and can change their mind at any time. Always try to collect other forms of evidence.

3.   Physical Evidence from the Harasser. In some instances, harassers communicate with their victims using written notes or letters, e-mail messages, or phone messages left on answering machines. Be sure to save anything that confirms the harasser's contact and communication with you. Such tangible or physical evidence can be absolutely invaluable in documenting your complaint!

4.   Tape Recording. In the overwhelming majority of all cases, the initial incident of faculty sexual harassment is completely unexpected by the victim, catching her "off-guard" and unprepared to immediately begin evidence collection. However, if you anticipate that the harassment will continue, and it often does, covertly tape recording future conversations can provide devastating, indisputable evidence to support your case. Technology exists to reliably match a person's voice with that on a tape.

Taping the harasser in action is the "ultimate" proof of his unlawful behavior. While taping, you can also verbally review earlier harassing incidents and solicit comments or confirmation from the professor to document their occurrence.

Microcassette recorders and tapes are readily available at any retailer selling electronic equipment. They can be easily concealed in a pocket or purse and can reliably record conversations lasting up to 45 minutes without flipping the tape.

Specific retailers, model names and numbers, and prices include:

1.   Walmart, GE Microcassette Recorder with Clip-On Microphone (#3-5375), $25.47.
2.   Circuit City, Sony Microcassette Recorder (#M430), $29.99.

Quality micro tapes can be purchased at Sears: 4-pack of Panasonic Micro Tapes, 30 minutes per side for $4.99; 4-pack of Sony Micro Tapes, 45 minutes per side for $6.99 or Circuit City: 3-packof TDK tapes, 45 minutes per side for $5.99.

We have found that tape recording perpetrators in action is a particularly powerful way of proving your case. Thus, we highly recommend that you consider using this method of collecting evidence.

5.   Phone Recording. Before using this approach, be sure to check with a local attorney to determine if you can legally tape record a telephone conversation in your state, if the other party is unaware that taping is occurring. Laws differ from one state to the next and it is important to confirm what statutes apply to you.

If taping is legal, recording phone conversations with the harassing professor can provide compelling evidence of his unlawful conduct. You can also use this technology to place a phone call to the professor to review earlier harassing incidents or untaped conversations and solicit his comments as documentation of their existence.

The equipment needed to tape phone conversations can be purchased from major electronics retailers. Installation is typically quite simple and straightforward. Once operational, you can record any incoming or outgoing call. In the absence of highly sophisticated detection equipment, the harasser would have no idea that taping was occurring.

Two possible equipment choices include:

1. Radio Shack, Microcassette Phone Recorder (#43-476), $79.99.
2. Gadget Universe, www.gadgetuniverse.com, 8-hour Telephone Recorder (#TP802), $119.95.

6. Video Recording. If the harassing professor's behaviors can be videotaped, this type of evidence can provide indisputable support for your complaint. For example, if a harasser tells you that he will drop by your apartment to discuss your course grade and how to improve it, the opportunity to collect videotape evidence exists.

This can be accomplished in a number of ways. First you could ask a trusted friend to videotape some or all of the interaction from a hidden position. Second, you could conceal a VCR in your living room area and turn it on just before the professor arrives.

A third option involves using a mini-camcorder the size of a pen to videotape the professor. Two excellent choices include:

1. Best Buy, Aiptek PenCam, $79.99.
2. The Sharper Image, Digi Pen Digital Camera (#AR850), $99.95.

7. Graduates and/or Former Students. Faculty harassers are often habitual sexual predators. In other words, they have repeatedly violated student rights for years. To the extent that this is true, there are likely to be many other victims, some of whom may be willing to file a complaint in support of yours. These women could include graduates who have completed their degrees and/or former students who have not yet finished their coursework or dropped out of school.

Locating and contacting women who have had harassing experiences similar to yours can be very challenging. Don't expect any help from the university. In fact, their attitude typically is, "if there was no complaint filed, no civil rights violation occurred," and "a silent victim is not a victim." This type of morally bankrupt, self-serving thinking continues in spite of research evidence indicating that only 2%

to 3% of women students who are harassed actually file a formal complaint.

If your complaint ever goes to court, your attorney may be successful in forcing the university to provide you with the names and addresses of former students who had classes with the harassing professor. This would significantly simplify the task of identifying and locating them.

Obtaining signed statements from other women who were harassed by the same professor can provide you with powerful evidence to support your complaint. In most instances, you will find that graduates are more willing to come forward because the threat of academic retaliation is not present.

For example, several years ago a female medical school student filed a formal sexual harassment complaint against an M.D. on the faculty alleging a "grades for sex" proposition. It was a classic case of "he said, she said" and the university was unwilling to thoroughly investigate the professor's behavior by contacting former students. Thus, the complaint resulted in no disciplinary action taken against the professor or compensation for the student victim.

Frustrated about the entire situation, the young woman searched for other ways to collect supporting evidence. Since she had heard rumors about this professor for years, she decided to personally write to female graduates of the medical school program to inquire about their interaction with this professor. If they had been harassed, the student asked them to put their experiences in writing and send a letter to the university (with a copy to her).

Six young M.D.s wrote letters detailing the sordid behavior of the professor in demanding sex for passing grades while they were students. In view of this additional confirmatory evidence, the university finally acted to terminate the professor.

While the harassing faculty member in the above case was ultimately removed from his position, the university itself had been unwilling to conduct a thorough, rigorous investigation after receiving the initial complaint. Once again, we painfully observe that universities are more interested in protecting professors than student civil rights.

Conclusions and a Final Note of Encouragement

Don't allow faculty harassers to violate your civil rights, and at the same time intimidate you from collecting evidence and filing a complaint against them. Stick up for yourself and fight back! With the right kind of documentation and evidence you can be successful.

CHAPTER 9

Surviving and Coping with an Experience

of Academic Sexual Harassment

Erin was an enthusiastic new student in her first semester at the college of her dreams. Two months into the term, she was victimized by a very brazen computer science professor, who sexually propositioned her in his office. Totally shocked and offended, Erin immediately rejected his advance. He quickly responded with an aggressive threat to give her an "F" for the class, which could result in academic probation and ultimately dismissal. With a sinister look on his face and glaring stare, the professor warned her of grave consequences if she told anyone about what happened saying, "You'll pay, I promise you, you'll pay."

As Erin left the professor's office, she was overwhelmed with feelings of rage, fear, frustration, and uncertainty. Upon returning to her room, Erin's dorm mate, Sally, could sense that something was seriously wrong. After reluctantly sharing parts of her experience, Sally encouraged Erin to go to the Dean of Student's Office just to find out what her options were—not necessarily to file a complaint because she could see that Erin was deeply concerned about the professor's threat.

Sally accompanied Erin to the Dean's office, where they made an appointment to see a counselor. While briefly explaining the reason for her visit, the intake secretary interrupted Erin and said, "I'll bet I know who you're talking about and what happened!"

Erin sat in stunned silence while the secretary told her, "off the record of course", that student complaints were received every semester about a certain professor in computer science, who was notorious for propositioning and sexually exploiting new students. She went on to say that even though several formal complaints had been filed, the university never took any action because the evidence was always of the "he said, she said" nature and because the professor was a world famous expert on emerging computer technologies and had attracted a multi-million dollar grant for the university.

After hearing this discouraging information, Erin decided to leave the office and cancelled her appointment. She then called her parents and they urged her to come home as soon as possible. Erin packed up and left that evening.

She was relieved to be in familiar territory again. It was great to see her mom, dad, and two brothers. Their caring, nurturing, and concern were just what she needed.

Unfortunately, Erin had a lot of trouble sleeping and endured terrifying nightmares of the professor stalking and attacking her. She began to worry constantly about what would happen to her and how she would ever continue her education. Gradually, a deep paralyzing depression set in and Erin refused to leave the house.

With her parents support, she wrote a letter to the university registrar and dropped all of her classes. She refused to mention the real reason for fear of retaliation from the professor.

At her mother's urging, Erin agreed to visit their family doctor and ask for something to help her sleep. After hearing her story, the physician recognized the potential severity of the psychological problems Erin was experiencing and referred her to a talented clinical psychologist, specializing in treating sexual abuse and harassment victims. The doctor also prescribed a mild sedative to help her fall asleep.

Erin was able to schedule a priority appointment the following day with the psychologist and liked her very much. For the next two months, Erin saw her therapist twice weekly. In collaboration with her family doctor, Erin also began taking an anti-depressant. During her therapy sessions, Erin began to explore what happened to her, how she felt about it, and possible actions/plans to deal with it and move on. The combination of better sleep, easing depression, productive therapy sessions, and a supportive family resulted in dramatic improvements in Erin's mental, emotional, and physical health. Together with her therapist and parents, Erin decided to file a formal complaint against the professor.

After the university refused to take any corrective action, Erin initiated a civil lawsuit. She endured a grueling, insulting deposition and two years of protracted legal maneuvering before finally winning a substantial six-figure, out-of-court settlement with the institution.

While the legal battle was still ongoing, Erin applied to and was accepted by Carnegie-Mellon University. Given her interest in computer science, she was convinced the CMU was a much better choice than her original one. Four years later, Erin graduated with honors and accepted a software programming position with Microsoft.

Erin's story above had a happy ending. She was very fortunate to have an understanding, supportive family with access to the kinds of resources she needed to recover. Erin fully utilized those resources and was able to work through what happened and move on with her life.

Unfortunately, most victims of academic sexual harassment, numbering in the millions, suffer in silence. They either don't have access to the support resources they need or don't use them. Failing to resolve their horrible experience at the hands of faculty sexual predators, many of these unfortunate women carry lifelong wounds that never heal and continue to disrupt their lives.

The primary purpose of this chapter is to clearly communicate that victims of academic sexual harassment can fully recover. There is hope and there is life after such a traumatizing experience. Ultimately, success in this endeavor involves a three-step process. First, it is important to understand and acknowledge the seriousness of what has happened to you, the potentially crippling short- and long-term consequences, and the critical need to find professional assistance.

The second step involves the search for qualified mental health professionals to guide and nurture your recovery. Finally, the third step entails an active commitment on your part to work with your counselor/therapist to achieve a full or nearly full recovery and return to a "normal life." We will discuss each of these three steps in more detail below.

Step 1—Understand and Acknowledge the Impact

As we emphasized in Chapter 1, sexual harassment often has a devastating impact on student victims. Serious symptoms and consequences can develop in three major areas: psychological, physical/medical, and behavioral/academic. Taken together, these symptoms can destroy a women's life and undermine her ability to function normally.

Further compounding the damage to victims are a number of self-defeating thought patterns and feelings that often arise. These include:

- an overwhelming sense of helplessness, hopelessness, and vulnerability
- devaluing one's self-worth and legitimate rights as a human being, student, and consumer
- an intense sense of personal guilt, responsibility, and shame for what happened
- a lack of confidence in one's perception or interpretation of the experience
- an overemphasis on the interests and rights of the faculty sexual predator
- strong fears about not being believed if the incident is reported, what the professor will do next, and possible retaliation
- denial or minimization of what actually happened

Clearly, the impact of sexual harassment on victims must be taken very seriously. Our advice to all victims is clear and unequivocal—seek professional assistance! You owe it to yourself to find a competent mental health practitioner to conduct a thorough evaluation and assessment. Early detection of potential problems is critical to successful treatment.

Help is available and even the most serious problems can be effectively treated. Don't risk your mental, emotional, and physical health!

Step 2—Finding Qualified Professional Assistance

In the aftermath of a sexual harassment encounter, a variety of people can be instrumental in helping you to recover. These include your parents, other relatives, close friends, supportive faculty, academic advisors, and clergy members.

Of paramount importance however is finding a qualified mental health professional to thoroughly assess the psychological/emotional damage you may have suffered and guide your recovery. Perhaps an analogy can best convey why this is so essential.

Let's assume that you were in a very serious automobile accident and suffered a deep, profusely bleeding cut to your abdomen. It is probably safe to say that you wouldn't dream of taking care of the injury yourself. Nor would you, in all likelihood, ask a parent, friend, relative or anyone without medical training to treat your wound.

What might happen if you did try to treat yourself or allow a non-professional to do it? What if the wound were not properly cleaned and sutured? What if you were not evaluated for internal bleeding or potential damage to vital organs? What if you were not monitored for possible infection and treated with antibiotics if one occurred? The answers to these questions are quite obvious—serious medical complications and even death could arise if the wound were not professionally evaluated and treated.

In a similar manner, sexual harassment can cause devastating psychological damage to an individual that is not immediately apparent to the victim herself or others without the appropriate professional training and experience. Thus, it is imperative, in our opinion that every victim of faculty sexual harassment obtain: (a) a thorough assessment of any psychological injuries and (b) a comprehensive treatment plan to repair those damages.

In a "best case scenario," psychological damage may be minimal or nonexistent. In these instances, there might be no need for a treatment plan or continuing therapy and the patient may be simply asked to schedule a follow-up appointment in 30 to 90 days to insure that everything is still fine.

On the other hand, in especially egregious cases, the trauma can be horrific, resulting in devastating psychological and physical symptoms. In these instances, effective treatment plans could take years to successfully execute.

We hope that we have made a strong and compelling argument for the vital necessity of enlisting the services of a qualified mental health professional when dealing with sexual harassment. You owe it to yourself! Don't jeopardize your emotional, mental, or physical health! Get the help you need.

Who Qualifies as a Mental Health Professional

There are three categories of mental health providers that have the necessary professional training and experience to effectively treat victims of sexual harassment: (1) psychiatrists, (2) clinical psychologists, and (3) clinical social workers. Professionals in all three of these categories are required to pass licensing exams in the state(s) in which they practice.

Psychiatrists are medical doctors (M.D.s) who have advanced specialized education and training in dealing with psychological disorders. Clinical psychologists typically possess one of two closely related types of doctoral degrees—a Ph.D. or a Psy.D. In both cases, there is comprehensive education and training in treating psychological problems. Finally, clinical social workers generally have a master's degree or MSW, entailing extensive psychological education and training. Individuals in any of these three categories are potential candidates to provide professional treatment to victims of sexual harassment. Additional steps involved in locating a therapist who is right for you are discussed below.

Conducting Your Search

One of the best ways to find a good therapist is through referrals from trusted sources. These could include family member, close friends, coworkers, clergy, supportive professors, family physician, women's rights groups, and women's support groups and shelters.

Ask each referral source for the names of two to three competent therapists in your vicinity. If you hear the same recommendations repeatedly from different sources, these are individuals worthy of further consideration.

You can also find qualified therapists by contacting local hospitals and community mental health centers. They can provide referrals to mental health professionals who are on the staff at their institution.

If all else fails, you can always consult the yellow pages or web directories to locate therapists. Using this approach requires more effort in evaluating their professional credentials and experience.

Regardless of how you locate a potential therapist, it is critical for you to assess her/his suitability for your case. The first step is to contact your state's professional licensing board to: (a) confirm a therapist's license status, and (b) inquire about misconduct/malpractice complaints and disciplinary history (not all states will provide this information to the public).The last thing a traumatized student victim needs is a therapist with a prior disciplinary record for sexually abusing clients.

If your therapist candidate is properly licensed and has a clean disciplinary record, we recommend calling her/his office to determine whether treating sexual harassment victims is an area of specialty. If the answer is "yes," schedule an initial appointment.

When you meet the therapist for the first time, it is important for you to continue your assessment of her/his suitability by asking questions concerning prior experience with sexual harassment victims, recommended psychological evaluation, typical treatment plan and duration, and success rates. If you receive appropriate answers and you're comfortable with the therapist—congratulations, this person could be invaluable in guiding your recovery.

On the other hand, if you don't like the therapist's answers or don't feel comfortable with her/him, exercise your consumer rights and continue the search process. Try not to get discouraged, you'll eventually find just the right therapist!

<u>University Counselors</u>

Most universities offer free counseling services to students. While many campus counselors are competent, caring professionals, we recommend that you find a therapist who is not affiliated with the university. Our primary rationale for this advice concerns the potential conflict of interest confronting any university-paid therapist.

There is a natural tendency on the part of an employee to protect the interests of her/his employer. A serious problem can arise when your interests as a student victim are contrary to the institution's interests. The dilemma facing a university therapist is whose interests are more important.

This dilemma comes into sharp focus if a university therapist is called to testify in court, on your behalf, against the institutions. We strongly recommend that you avoid such conflicted situations by choosing a therapist who has no formal connection to the university.

Cost of Therapy

Therapy sessions with qualified, experienced mental health professionals can be very expensive, ranging from a low of $75.00 per session to a high of $200.00 or more. Most health insurance plans cover all or some portion of these expenses. Also, many employers provide free counseling to employees and their families through EAPs (Employee Assistance Programs).

If you do not have health insurance and are unable to pay for therapy, there are several other available options. First, based upon your income and financial status, you may qualify for MEDICAID—a federal program to provide basic medical services to economically disadvantaged individuals. Second, you may qualify for indigent care at local state-supported hospitals and/or mental health centers. Third, you may qualify for a wide variety of non-profit victim assistance programs (a call to your local United Way can be very helpful in identifying these agencies).

It is essential that you get the professional assistance that you need. There are many organizations that can help and your challenge is to find and engage them.

Ultimately, the costs for your therapy and your pain and suffering should be borne by the harasser and his university. If they are unwilling to voluntarily pay your expense, legal action in civil court is your only recourse. Stand up for yourself and your rights. You shouldn't have to pay to recover from damage inflicted by a faculty sexual predator!

Step 3—Participation in the Recovery Process

Success in recovering as a victim of sexual harassment will require your active participation. You will need to work together with your therapist to effectively implement her/his treatment plan. Depending upon the nature and severity of your symptoms, the treatment plan could involve a number of activities or strategies.

First, you may be asked to schedule frequent office visits, over a period of several weeks or months. Second, you may be referred to medical specialists for treatment of physical problems, such as digestive disorders or high blood pressure. Third, you may be required to take medication for depression, anxiety, or stress.

Fourth, you may be asked to keep a journal of your thoughts and feelings about your experience. Fifth, you may be introduced to new ways to reframe/conceptualize what happened and asked to use them. Sixth, you may receive instruction on stress management techniques and encouraged to utilize them on a daily basis.

Ultimately, a successful recovery will allow you to clearly understand, acknowledge, cope with, and move on from your sexual harassment experience. Critical to this success is an ongoing, positive, self-affirming internal dialogue that: (1) validates your self-worth as a human being, (2) emphasizes your legitimate rights as a student and consumer, (3) clearly places responsibility for the harassing behavior on the professor, (4) identifies multiple options for dealing with the experience, (5) empowers effective responses, (6) enhances the attainment of closure on what happened, and (7) facilitates continuation with your life and a return to normal functioning.

Successful recovery is not possible without your full, active involvement and participation. You must be motivated to recover and willing to invest the necessary time, energy, and resources. Make that commitment and start the process.

Conclusions

Being victimized by a faculty sexual predator can be a horrific experience, with potentially devastating, lifelong consequences. Serious psychological, physical/medical and behavioral/academic symptoms can arise that require treatment by a qualified mental health professional.

If you have suffered an experience of sexual harassment, you owe it to yourself to seek the necessary professional evaluation and treatment. Guided by a competent therapist, your active commitment and involvement can result in solutions to even the most serious problems.

You need and deserve a full recovery, so move forward and make it happen! Try to view what occurred as a learning experience, however painful, that will make you a stronger person, enable you to help others, and motivate you to aggressively fight academic sexual harassment! Good luck in this process.

CHAPTER 10

Fighting Back—Specific Strategies to

Combat Sexual Harassment on Campus

A life sciences professor with a prior disciplinary record for sexual harassment that involved creating a hostile, intimidating, sexually offensive learning environment in his classroom had received a token, slap-on-the-wrist punishment and continued teaching—a disgusting, yet typical response from university administrators. Within a short period of time, he committed an unthinkable act in class—sexually disfiguring a cadaver and then making offensive comments and jokes about this act.

Written student complaints led to an internal investigation that resulted in another slap-on-the-wrist punishment. Once again, he was allowed to continue teaching.

Shocking and outrageous conduct by faculty harassers like this does occur in academia. Equally as reprehensibly is the typically spineless response by university administrators who allow such predators to remain in the classroom and essentially go unpunished.

After observing this phenomena occur again, and again, and again, we have come to the firm conclusion that universities and their faculties are both unwilling and unable to effectively stop the problem of sexual harassment on campus. We have given-up trying to work with them to bring about internal reforms to solve the problem. The harassers and their "good-old-boy- network" are simply too entrenched, too powerful, and too intimidating for serious internal reform to occur. Addressing this issue in Forbes magazine (September 7, 1998), Thomas Sowell (an economist and senior fellow at the Hoover Institution in Stanford, CA) stated: "The likelihood that the academic world will reform itself from within is about the same as the likelihood that the Mafia will decide to go straight."

We are convinced that the only way to solve the academic sexual harassment problem is to mobilize external forces to compel universities to make the necessary reforms. This can be done by educating and empowering students and their parents as consumers with a legitimate set of specific rights. It can also be done by appealing to individuals and organizations that accredit, regulate, fund, evaluate, and support university operations.

In this chapter, we will present a set of recommendations concerning how you and others can exert external pressures on universities to aggressively protect student civil rights and stop faculty sexual harassment. We will discuss these strategies in two major categories—on-campus and off-campus. Our lists are not exhaustive, so we encourage you and others to formulate additional creative ways to influence university behavior.

On-Campus Strategies

Write to University President. Before enrolling or reenrolling at a university, write (either you or your parents) to the President and request a written response to the following items:

1. Campus sexual harassment/sexual misconduct statistics for the last 5 years.
2. Certification that no teaching faculty or student advisors at the institution have a prior disciplinary record for sexual harassment/sexual misconduct involving students or a list of faculty and advisors who do not have a prior record.
3. Certification that the Student Bill of Rights contained in Chapter 5 would be honored at the institution.
4. Results of an independent evaluation of the institution's sexual harassment prevention efforts, using a tool like the survey in Chapter 5.

If the university President fails to respond (don't be too surprised) or the response is unacceptable, exercise your right as a consumer and take your business/tuition dollars elsewhere to an institution more respectful of your civil and consumer rights. It might also be helpful to share your experience and the President's response, or lack thereof, with the campus student newspaper and local news media.

Faculty Disclosure Form. You, your parents, or better yet, the student government can send the Disciplinary Disclosure Form (see Chapter 6) to campus faculty and ask that they complete and return it. Only take classes from those professors without a prior disciplinary record for sexual harassment/sexual misconduct who are willing to respect your civil and consumer rights!

Sexual Harassment Prevention Training. Submit a written request to university administration to provide mandatory comprehensive training in sexual harassment prevention to all students, faculty, and staff. If you receive a negative or unacceptable response, share it with campus and local media.

Sexual Harassment Incidence Survey. Submit a written request to the university administration to administer a standardized Sexual Harassment Incidence Survey to a large random sample of campus students and publish the results in the student newspaper, along with an action plan to address any problem areas.

Pro-Student Speakers. Invite pro-student speakers to campus to discuss and highlight the problem of academic sexual harassment and how to prevent it.

Student Support Group. Establish a student-organized support group, independent of the university, to assist victims of faculty sexual harassment in getting the help and advice they need to effectively cope and respond.

Student Government Activism. Encourage the student government at your institution to become actively involved in this critical issue. Elected student representatives can and should press university officials to move effectively to protect student civil rights.

Supportive Faculty. While most faculty are supportive of efforts to prevent academic sexual harassment, very few are willing to get directly and personally involved—often due to fear of academic/professional or personal retaliation from harassers and/or their supporters. Nevertheless, the support of a bold faculty member or members can be invaluable in prodding the institution to improve its preventive efforts. We wholeheartedly believe that professors have a moral and professional responsibility to vigorously protect student civil rights. Supportive faculty can perform a number of specific useful functions, including: (a) filing sexual harassment complaints on behalf of students with the Office for Civil Rights (OCR) of the Department of Education, (b) providing information to students about prevention, (c) offering assistance and encouragement to student victims, (d) testifying against harassers and universities in court cases, (e) writing articles for the campus newspaper, (f) and conducting surveys of the incidence of student sexual harassment on campus.

Don't be afraid to confront potentially supportive faculty members and assertively request their assistance. Those professors who won't help you and won't fight vigorously to protect student civil rights at their institution should find another vocation. By refusing to be part of the solution, they become part of the problem.

Off-Campus Strategies

There are a number of ways to bring powerful external pressures to bear on universities to improve their sexual harassment prevention efforts. The most promising stakeholders and strategies are described below.

State/Federal Lawmakers. Members of state and/or federal legislatures could be contacted to solicit their active involvement. For example, they could be asked to initiate state or federal investigations into the magnitude and nature of the sexual harassment problem on U.S. campuses.

Additionally, lawmakers could be encouraged to enact supportive legislation in the areas mentioned below. Unsympathetic or unresponsive officials could be voted out at the next election.

1. require universities to publish campus harassment statistics, just as they are now required to publish campus crime statistics by the federal government,
2. require universities receiving state or federal funding to pass an annual comprehensive review of their sexual harassment prevention efforts, using an instrument like the one presented in Chapter 5,
3. expand the operating budget for the Office for Civil Rights (OCR) and increase its power to discipline institutions that violate student civil rights,
4. criminalize sexual relations between professors and their students (even if consensual), as some states have done with therapists and clergy and the people they counsel,
5. override the recent 1998 Supreme Court ruling that relieved universities of liability in student sexual harassment cases unless it

could be proved that the institution acted with "deliberate indifference" when a complaint was properly filed,

6. require that faculty disciplinary records concerning sexual harassment/sexual misconduct involving students be available for public review,

7. establish a student bill of rights (see Chapter 5), similar to the recently enacted patients bill of rights in healthcare,

8. create a state/national registry of faculty sexual harassers to avoid the problem of hiring a professor who was previously fired for sexual harassment,

9. require that all entering students receive full and complete information/education about academic sexual harassment,

10. prevent faculty with disciplinary records for sexual harassment/sexual misconduct involving students from continuing to teach,

11. require universities to use comprehensive psychological screening and background checks when hiring professors and administrators,

12. require that cases involving alleged faculty sexual harassment be heard and decided by an independent, specially trained panel of civil court judges.

Although it is beyond the scope of this book, we strongly believe that many of these legislative recommendations should also be applied to institutions providing pre-school and kindergarten through grade 12 education. Students in these settings are even more vulnerable and at-risk than those in college.

Government Oversight and Enforcement Agencies. There are multiple governmental agencies/offices at both the federal and state levels that could potentially be helpful in protecting student civil and consumer rights. For example, they include: the Office for Civil Rights (OCR) at the U.S. Department of Education, the U.S. Justice Department, the U.S. Attorney General, the U.S. Consumer Protection Agency, and state attorneys general. Requests for support and specific action could be directed to administrators in these agencies/offices. If an acceptable response is not forthcoming, the matter could then be referred to the appropriate legislative oversight committee.

Women's and Civil Rights Groups. You could solicit support for your campus efforts from a variety of powerful women's and civil rights groups, including the American Association of University Women (AAUW), the National Organization for Women (NOW), the National Association for the Advancement of Colored People (NAACP), and Reverend Jackson's Rainbow

Coalition. These groups could be instrumental in focusing media and national attention on the problem and how to solve it.

Consumer Rights Groups. There are countless consumer rights groups at the state and national level that should enthusiastically support efforts to protect student rights as consumers of higher education. Two specific examples are the Better Business Bureau and Ralph Nader's Consumer Advocate Center.

Alumni Groups. University alumni associations offer an interesting opportunity to influence institutional policies and programs. As graduates, alumni have a vested interest in maintaining the status and prestige of their alma mater. Perhaps more importantly, they are a critical source of financial contributions. Alumni groups could be invited to join the efforts to prevent sexual harassment on campus and influence administrators to cooperate, or withhold donations.

Wealthy Donors. Every university has a set of wealthy individuals who regularly donate substantial sums to the institution. These individuals could be contacted and informed of the disgraceful problem of sexual harassment on campus. They could be encouraged to influence administrators, and ultimately withhold donations if meaningful reforms were not implemented.

Educational Foundations. Each year many universities receive substantial financial grants from literally hundreds of educational foundations. Two prominent examples are the Ford Foundation and the Lilly Foundation. These organizations could require that universities pass an annual comprehensive review of their sexual harassment prevention efforts (using an instrument like the one in Chapter 5) before funds are awarded.

Accreditation Agencies. Within the U.S. higher education system, accreditation agencies have been established to determine quality standards and regularly review universities to insure that the standards are being met. These agencies consist of those that accredit an overall institution (like the North Central Association for schools in the upper Midwest) or professional schools within an institution, including business, nursing, and education.

Achieving and maintaining accreditation is of paramount importance to most universities. Using this powerful leverage, accrediting agencies could be encouraged to set rigorous standards for sexual harassment prevention and include them in their regular review process. Institutions that could not pass a comprehensive assessment of their prevention efforts should not be accredited or reaccredited.

College Rating Services. Organizations that provide ratings of U.S. colleges could be asked to include an assessment of institutional success in preventing academic sexual harassment. Thus, the popular U.S. News and World Report Guide to America's Best Colleges could provide evaluations, not only of academic quality, but also of institutional commitment to protecting student civil and consumer rights.

Parents Groups. Parents certainly have a vested interest in protecting their children's civil rights. Organizations at the high school level, like the Parent Teacher Association (PTA), could be contacted for their support in prevention efforts. Specifically, in conjunction with high school administrators and teachers, efforts could be initiated to inform and educate college-bound students about the problem of academic sexual harassment and how to avoid it— hopefully helping them become "harassment-proof" before they start college. Also, policies could be developed to allow recruiting visits only from those universities that pass an annual comprehensive review of their sexual harassment prevention efforts.

We know of one organization that specifically represents parents of university students— College Parents of America (www.collegeparents.org). This group should certainly be interested in supporting efforts to prevent academic sexual harassment.

Innovative Lawsuits. We encourage students and their attorneys to try innovative lawsuits as a way to force institutions to protect student civil rights. Specifically, we believe that the area of consumer fraud holds interesting possibilities. For example, before purchasing a house or used car, the seller is legally required to provide full disclosure of any defects. Shouldn't such basic protection also apply to students who purchase an educational service from universities? We certainly believe so and contend that the overwhelming majority of students would not enroll in classes offered by convicted harassers!

Perhaps the most compelling argument for consumer fraud occurs when a faculty member with a prior disciplinary record for harassment continues to prey on unsuspecting, uninformed students. Clearly, a knowingly "defective product" was offered for sale with reckless disregard for the potential damage to the customer.

Business executives who willfully allow this to happen often face criminal prosecution. We feel that this is certainly appropriate for university administrators who allow known harassers, often with extensive disciplinary records, to continue teaching and unlawfully violating student civil rights.

We also strongly believe that this type of conduct on the part of university administrators exceeds the Supreme Court's definition of "deliberate indifference" to complaints of sexual harassment and exposes students to unreasonable risks on campus. We encourage attorneys for student victims to use this concept as an operational definition for "deliberate indifference" and are confident that most juries would agree and respond favorably.

Media. Unfortunately, universities have done a great job concealing the problem of sexual harassment on campus. Consequently, the general public is typically unaware of its existence and certainly has no idea about its magnitude or severity. To address this lack of awareness, we need to involve the media—newspapers, magazines, radio, television, websites—in focusing public attention on the problem and galvanizing support for prevention efforts. Universities absolutely abhor negative publicity. It's bad for their image, enrollment, and fundraising. Consequently, institutions often respond quickly and decisively to a concerted public outcry about a particular issue.

In addition to highlighting problem areas, media attention should also be directed to those universities that are successfully preventing harassment on campus. The "favorable press" should enhance their image, enrollment, and fundraising.

Conclusions

The lawless conduct of faculty sexual predators has continued unabated for decades. Their ruthless and brazen violations of fundamental student civil rights demonstrate an utter disregard and disrespect for their victims. Administrators who have allowed the harassers to operate with near impunity are accessories to these atrocities. In our opinion, both faculty sexual predators and cowardly administrators need to be banished from higher education.

Successfully addressing this problem will require bold, aggressive, forceful action—the only message that harassers and weak-willed administrators understand. This is not a task for the faint of heart. It requires courageous, committed individuals who will lead an unrelenting attack on the culprits and their supporters. We encourage you and others to join us in this fight. We hope that the recommended strategies we have discussed in this chapter will be helpful in focusing and mobilizing your efforts. Let's join together and remove this scourge from academia. Remember: <u>One more victim is one too many!</u>

Appendix A

Selected References and Resources

Selected References

The following selected references can provide a great deal of important additional information about the topic of sexual harassment in higher education:

1. AAUW Legal Advocacy Fund (2000) A License for Bias: Sex, Schools, and Title IX, Washington, D.C.: AAUW Legal Advocacy Fund.
2. Brandenburg, J. B. (1997) Confronting Sexual Harassment: What Schools and Colleges Can Do, New York: Teachers College Press.
3. Dziech, B. W. & Weiner, L. (1984) The Lecherous Professor, Boston: Beacon Press.
4. Dziech, B. W. & Weiner, L. (1990) The Lecherous Professor—Sexual Harassment on Campus (2nd ed.) Chicago: University of Illinois Press.
5. Fitzgerald, L. F. (1992) Sexual Harassment in Higher Education: Concepts & Issues, Washington, D.C.: National Education Association.
6. Hobson, C. J. & Guziewicz, J. (in press) Sexual Harassment Preventive and Protective Practices at U.S. Colleges and Universities, College Student Affairs Journal.
7. Katz, M. & Vieland, V. (1993) Get Smart (2nd ed.), New York: The Feminist Press.
8. Oppedisano, J. (1997) Academics' Shame: Our Failure to Confront Sexual Harassment, NWSA Journal, 9, No. 2, 126-234.
9. Paludi, M. A. (1996) Sexual Harassment on College Campuses— Abusing the Ivory Power (revised ed.), Albany, NY: State University of New York Press.
10. Sandler, B. R. & Shoop, R. J. (1997) Sexual Harassment on Campus— A Guide for Administrators, Faculty, and Students. Boston: Allyn and Bacon.
11. Schulhofer, S. J. (1998) Unwanted Sex—The Culture of Intimidation and the Failure of Law, Cambridge, MA: Harvard University Press.
12. Thompson Publishing Group. (1998) Educator's Guide to Controlling Sexual Harassment, Washington D.C.: Thompson Publishing Group.

13.   U.S. Department of Education (2001) Office of Civil Rights (Revised)
        Sexual Harassment Guidance: Harassment of Students by School
        Employees, Other Students, or Third Parties, 66 Federal Register 5512,
        Jan 19, 2001.

Selected Resources

1.   National and Regional Offices of the Office for Civil Rights
        National Office
        U.S. Department of Education
        Office for Civil Rights
        Mary E. Switzer Bldg.
        330 C St. SW
        Washington, D.C. 20202
        Phone: (800) 421-3481
        Fax: (202) 205-9862
        TDD: (202) 205-5166
        Email: OCR@ed.gov
        Homepage: http://www.ed.gov/offices/OCR/

        Eastern Division
        Connecticut, Maine, Massachusetts, New Hampshire, Rhode Island,
        Vermont
        Office for Civil Rights, Boston Office
        U.S. Department of Education
        J.W. McCormack Post Office & Courthouse, Rm. 707
        Boston, MA 02109-4557
        Phone: (617) 223-9662
        Fax: (617) 223-9669
        TDD: (617) 223-9695
        Email: OCR_Boston@ed.gov

        New Jersey, New York, Puerto Rico, Virgin Islands
        Office for Civil Rights, New York Office
        U.S. Department of Education
        75 Park Pl. 14th Floor
        New York, NY 10007-2146
        Phone: (212) 637-6466
        Fax: (212) 264-3803

TDD: (212) 637-0478
Email: OCR_NewYork@ed.gov

Delaware, Maryland, Kentucky, Pennsylvania, West Virginia
Office for Civil Rights, Philadelphia Office
U.S. Department of Education
Wanamaker Bldg., Ste. 515
100 Penn Square East
Philadelphia, PA 19107
Phone: (215) 656-8541
Fax: (215) 656-8605
TDD: (215) 656-8604
Email: OCR_Philadelphia@ed.gov

Southern Division
Alabama, Florida, Georgia, South Carolina, Tennessee
Office for Civil Rights, Atlanta Office
U.S. Department of Education
61 Forsyth St. SW
Atlanta, GA 30303-3104
Phone: (404) 562-6350
Fax: (404) 562-6455
TDD: (404) 331-7236
Email: OCR_Atlanta@ed.gov

Arkansas, Louisiana, Mississippi, Oklahoma, Texas
Office for Civil Rights, Dallas Office
U.S. Department of Education
1999 Bryan St. Ste. 2600
Dallas, TX 75201
Phone: (214) 880-2459
Fax: (214) 880-3082
TDD: (214) 880-2456
Email   OCR_Dallas@ed.gov

North Carolina, Virginia, Washington, D.C.
Office for Civil Rights, DC Office
U.S. Department of Education
1100 Pennsylvania Ave. NW, Rm. 316
P.O. Box 14620

Washington, DC 20044-4620
Phone: (202) 208-2545
Fax: (202) 208-7797
TDD: (202) 208-7741
Email: OCR_DC@ed.gov

Midwestern Division
Illinois, Indiana, Minnesota, Wisconsin
Office for Civil Rights, Chicago Office
U.S. Department of Education
111 N. Canal St. Ste. 1053
Chicago, IL 60606-7204
Phone: (312) 886-8434
Fax: (312) 353-4888
TDD: (312) 353-2540
Email: OCR_Chicago@ed.gov

Michigan and Ohio
Office for Civil Rights, Cleveland Office
U.S. Department of Education
600 Superior Ave. East
Bank One Ctr. Rm. 750
Cleveland, OH 44114-2611
Phone: (216) 522-4970
Fax: (216) 522-2573
TDD: (216) 522-4944
Email: OCR_Cleveland@ed.gov

Iowa, Kansas, Missouri, Nebraska, North Dakota, South Dakota
Office for Civil Rights, Kansas City Office
U.S. Department of Education
10220 N. Executive Hills Blvd. 8th Floor
Kansas City, MO 64153-1367
Phone: (816) 880-4200
Fax: (816) 891-0644
TDD: (816) 891-0582
Email: OCR_KansasCity@ed.gov

Western Division
Arizona, Colorado, Montana, New Mexico, Utah, Wyoming

Office for Civil Rights, Denver Office
U.S. Department of Education
Federal Bldg, St. 310
1244 Speer Boulevard
Denver, CO 80204-3582
Phone: (303) 844-5695
Fax: (303) 844-4303
TDD: (303) 844-3417
Email: OCR_Denver@ed.gov

California
Office for Civil Rights, San Francisco Office
U.S. Department of Education
Old Federal Bldg.
50 United Nations Plaza, Rm. 239
San Francisco, CA 94102-4102
Phone: (415) 556-4275
Fax: (415) 437-7786
TDD: (415) 437-7783
Email: OCR_SanFranscisco@ed.gov

Alaska, Hawaii, Idaho, Nevada, Oregon, Washington, American Samoa,
Guam, Pacific Islands
Office for Civil Rights, Seattle Office
U.S. Department of Education
915 Second Ave. Rm. 3310
Seattle, WA 98174-1099
Phone: (206) 220-7900
Fax: (206) 220-7887
TDD: (206) 220-7907
Email: OCR_Seattle@ed.gov

2.   American Association of University Women (AAUW), www.aauw.org

3.   National Organization for Women (NOW), www.now.org

4.   College Parents of America, www.collegeparents.org

Appendix B

UNIVERSITY SEXUAL HARASSMENT PREVENTION RATING SCALE©

An Assessment Guide for Students, Parents, Faculty and Administrators

UNIVERSITY SEXUAL HARASSMENT PREVENTION RATING SCALE©

1. <u>Formal Institutional Policies Related to Sexual Harassment</u>
    (10 possible points)

    _____   1 pt (1) Campus has a written policy prohibiting sexual harassment.

    _____   1 pt (2) Professors are prohibited from having sexual relationships with students whom they teach/supervise/oversee.

    _____   1 pt (3) The campus Affirmative Action Officer is a tenured full-professor who reports directly to the university President.

    _____   1 pt (4) All faculty members and administrators are required to report any incident of potential sexual harassment brought to their attention.

    _____   1 pt (5) Thorough background checks are conducted on all candidates for academic positions, to include investigating prior problems with sexual harassment.

    _____   2 pts (6) A written survey of campus sexual harassment is conducted annually.

_____   1 pt (7)   Students are represented on campus committees dealing with sexual harassment issues.

_____   1 pt (8)   Student evaluations of professors' classroom teaching include questions dealing with sexual harassment.

_____   1 pt (9)   Letters of reference for faculty who resign while under investigation for sexual harassment clearly indicate this fact.

Sub-Total Points

(also enter in the appropriate box on the scoring summary sheet – last page).

2. <u>Sexual Harassment Training/Education</u> (10 possible points)

   _____   4 pts   (1) <u>Mandatory</u> sexual harassment training/education for <u>all</u> faculty.

   _____   4 pts   (2) <u>Mandatory</u> sexual harassment training/education for <u>all</u> students.

   _____   1 pts   (3) <u>Mandatory</u> special training for academic administrators on their roles and responsibilities.

   _____   1 pts   (4) <u>Mandatory</u> sexual harassment training/education for <u>all</u> part-time/adjunct faculty and teaching lab assistants.

Sub-Total Points

(also enter in the appropriate box on the scoring summary sheet – last page).

3.   <u>Student Support Services</u> (10 possible points)

      _____   5 pts   (1) Student advocate or ombudsperson is available on campus.

      _____   3 pts   (2) Free professional counseling services are available to students.

      _____   1 pt   (3) 24-hour crisis hotline is available for student use.

      _____   1 pt   (4) Referral service to local mental health professionals is available to students.

      [ ]   Sub-Total Points

(also enter in the appropriate box on the scoring summary sheet – last page).

4.   <u>Complaint Processing and Investigations</u> (15 possible points)

_____   2 pts   (1) <u>All</u> complaints are investigated.

_____   2 pts   (2) Investigations are conducted by independent, <u>professionally-qualified</u> personnel.

_____   2 pts   (3) A central record is maintained of all complaints and resolution outcomes.

_____   2 pts   (4) For complaints alleging flagrant violations of student civil rights, the professor involved is suspended with pay from all student-contact activities, pending the results of a thorough investigation.

_____   2 pts   (5) Complaint investigation results are submitted to an independent, professionally-qualified review board (e.g., specially trained local judges) for recommended action.

_____   2 pts   (6) If an investigation produces evidence of a possible criminal violation, the case is submitted to the local prosecutor's office.

_____   1 pt   (7) Institutional complaints are filed by the university against professors

for whom multiple
informal/anonymous student
complaints have been received.

_____ 1 pt (8) Students who initiate a complaint with
the university are informed about <u>all</u> of
their filing options.

_____ 1 pt (9) When evaluating a complaint filed
against a particular professor, all
previous complaints and disciplinary
actions are fully reviewed.

Sub-Total Points

(also enter in the appropriate box on
the scoring summary sheet – last page).

5. <u>Complaint Resolution Outcomes for Students</u> (5 possible points)

_____   2 pts   (1) Harassed students receive tuition reimbursement for classes in which harassment occurred.

_____   2 pts   (2) Harassed students are given the option to transfer their scholarship/financial aid to another institution.

_____1 pt   (3) Harassed students receive a formal written apology from the university.

Sub-Total Points

(also enter in the appropriate box on the scoring summary sheet – last page).

6. Faculty Discipline (25 possible points)

_____   12 pts   (1) Documented harassers are strongly
                          disciplined (including: suspension
                          without pay; permanent cessation of
                          all student-contact activities;
                          mandatory counseling; termination)

_____   12 pts   (2) For repeated and/or flagrant
                          documented incidents of sexual
                          harassment, faculty are terminated.

_____   1 pt   (3) Professors who fail to attend
                          mandatory sexual harassment
                          training are formally disciplined.

Sub-Total Points

(also enter in the appropriate box on
the scoring summary sheet – last page).

7. <u>Public Reporting and Information Dissemination</u> (25 possible points)

    _____ 10 pts (1) Summary statistics on the incidence of campus sexual harassment are published annually, distributed throughout the institution, and provided to current and prospective students.

    _____ 5 pts (2) Summaries of individual sexual harassment complaints (to include: charges, findings, and actions taken, but no names of the persons involved) are published annually, distributed throughout the campus community, and provided to current and prospective students.

    _____ 5 pts (3) Prior to enrolling in specific classes, information is made available to students concerning faculty with prior disciplinary records for sexual harassment/sexual misconduct involving students.

    _____ 2 pts (4) Results of the annual campus sexual harassment survey are published in the student newspaper.

    _____ 1 pt (5) Information about how to use the institution's sexual harassment complaint processing system and

other filing options is mailed
annually to all students.

_____ 1 pt (6) Information about academic sexual
harassment, complaint procedures,
and filing options is included in all
major campus publications (e.g.,
class schedule, course catalog,
student handbook).

_____ 1 pt (7) Information about academic sexual
harassment, complaint procedures,
and filing options is publicly and
prominently posted throughout the
campus.

Sub-Total Points

(also enter in the appropriate box on
the scoring summary sheet – last page).

UNIVERSITY SEXUAL HARASSMENT PREVENTION RATING SCALE©

Scoring Summary Sheet

☐   1. Formal Institutional Policies (10 possible points)

☐   2. Sexual Harassment Training/Education (10 possible points)

☐   3. Student Support Service (10 possible points)

☐   4. Complaint Processing and Investigations (15 possible points)

☐   5. Complaint Resolution Outcomes for Students (5 possible points)

☐   6. Faculty Discipline (25 possible points)

☐   7. Public Reporting and Information Dissemination (25 possible points)

_____

☐ Total (100 possible points)

_____

Appendix C

U.S. Department of Education

Office for Civil Rights

DISCRIMINATION COMPLAINT FORM

This form is not required to file a complaint with the Office for Civil Rights (OCR); however, the information requested on items 1 through 7 and on item 12 must be provided in writing, whether or not the form is used. Please type or print all information and use additional pages if more space is needed.

1. Name of person filing this complaint:

    NAME (Mr./Ms.): _____

                      (Last)   (First)   (Middle)

    ADDRESS: _____

    CITY & STATE _____

                                       (Zip Code)

    PHONE NO: _____(Home)

                    (Area Code)   (Number)

                    _____(Work)

                    (Area Code)   (Number)

2. Name of person allegedly discriminated against (if other than person filing):

    NAME (Mr./Ms.): _____

                      (Last)   (First)   (Middle)

    ADDRESS: _____

    CITY & STATE _____

                                         (Zip Code)

THE LECHEROUS UNIVERSITY

PHONE NO: _____(Home)
                         (Area Code)   (Number)

                         _____(Work)
                         (Area Code)   (Number)

U.S. Department of Education   Discrimination Complaint Form
Office of Civil Rights

3.   OCR engages in resolution activities on discrimination complaints against
      institutions and agencies, which receive funds from the U.S.
      Department of Education. It also engages in such activities for certain
      public entities that are subject to the provisions of Title II of the
      Americans with Disabilities Act (ADA). Please identify the institution
      or agency that engaged in the alleged discrimination. If we cannot
      accept your complaint, we will attempt to refer it to the appropriate
      agency and will notify you of that fact.

      NAME OF INSTITUTION: _____

      ADDRESS: _____

      CITY & STATE: _____
                                                    (Zip Code)
      DEPT/SCHOOL: _____

      Please indicate the relationship of the person identified in item 2 to the
      above institution: student, employee or other (please specify) ____
      _____

4.   The regulations OCR enforces prohibit discrimination on the basis of race,
      color, national origin, sex, disability, and/or age. Please indicate the
      basis or bases for the discrimination alleged in this complaint:

      For example:

            Discrimination based on race: black;
            Discrimination based on disability: learning disability.

      _____

      _____

U.S. Department of Education   Discrimination Complaint Form
Office for Civil Rights

5.   Please describe the alleged discriminatory act(s). Please include the dates
     of the alleged discrimination, the names of persons involved and, as
     available, the names of any persons who witnessed the acts.

     _____

     _____

     _____

6.   Please state the facts, which you believe indicate that the acts were
     discriminatory on the basis or bases, you specified in item 4.

     _____

     _____

     _____

7.   What is the most recent date that the alleged discrimination occurred?

     _____

     If this date is more than 180 days ago, you may request a waiver of the
     filing requirement. Please do so here and explain why you waited until
     now to file your complaint.

     _____

     _____

     _____

     _____

CHARLES J. HOSBON Ph.D. & COLLEEN L. HOBSON, M.S., R.N. 167

U.S. Department of Education   Discrimination Complaint Form
Office for Civil Rights

8. Have you attempted to resolve the allegations contained in this complaint
    with the institution through an internal grievance procedure?

                YES _____   NO _____

    If you answered yes, please describe the allegations in your grievance,
    identify the date you filed your grievance, and tell us the status of the
    grievance. If possible, please provide us with a copy of your grievance
    filed with the institution and any responses from the institution.

    _____

    _____

    _____

9. If the allegations contained in this complaint have been filed with any other
    federal, state, or local agency, or any federal or state court, please
    give details and dates. We will determine whether it is appropriate to
    engage in complaint resolution activities based upon the specific
    allegations of your complaint and the actions taken by the other
    agency or court.

    AGENCY OR COURT: _____

    _____

    _____

    DATE FILED: _____

    CASE NUMBER OR REFERENCE: _____

    RESULTS OF INVESTIGATION/FINDINGS BY AGENCY OR
    COURT: _____
    _____
    _____

U.S. Department of Education   Discrimination Complaint Form
Office for Civil Rights

10.   If we cannot reach you at your home or work, we would like to have the
      name and telephone number of another person (relative or friend) who
      knows where and when we can reach you. This information is not
      required, but it will be helpful to us.

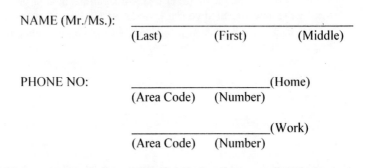

        NAME (Mr./Ms.):   _____
                             (Last)   (First)   (Middle)

        PHONE NO: _____(Home)
                             (Area Code)   (Number)

                             _____(Work)
                             (Area Code)   (Number)

11.   OCR has an expedited complaint resolution process called Early
      Complaint Resolution (ECR). In this process, we attempt to help the
      complainant and the institution reach an agreement through mediation
      to settle the complaint. Both the complainant and the institution must
      want to take part in the mediation. The complainant, the institution, or
      OCR may end the ECR process at any time if it appears that an
      agreement cannot be reached. If this happens, we will use other
      approaches to resolve the complaint allegations. One of the primary
      benefits of ECR is that it may be possible to resolve your complaint
      quickly. More information about the ECR process is contained in the
      enclosed document, "Information About OCR's Complaint Resolution
      Procedures."

      If OCR feels that mediation of your complaint is appropriate, are you
      interested in having OCR mediate your complaint?

      YES _____   NO _____

      If you answered yes and OCR determines ECR may be appropriate, we
      will contact you to discuss our ECR procedures in detail.

CHARLES J. HOSBON Ph.D. & COLLEEN L. HOBSON, M.S., R.N. 169

U.S. Department of Education　　　　　　　Discrimination Complaint Form
Office for Civil Rights

12.　We cannot accept your complaint if it has not been signed. Please sign and
　　　date your complaint below.

_____　　_____
　　(Date)　　　　　　　　　　　　　(Signature)

Please send us copies of any written materials or other documents, which
you think will help us understand your complaint.

Please mail the completed Discrimination Complaint Form to: The U.S.
Department of Education, Office for Civil Rights, Regional Office in
your area. Also, please enclose your signed consent form(s) with the
Discrimination Complaint Form. See "Information About OCR's
Complaint Resolution Procedures" for information about the consent
forms. If you have any questions about how to complete this form or
properly file your complaint, please call the appropriate regional office.
Thank you.

CONSENT FORM – COMPLAINANT

I have read the Office for Civil Rights (OCR) document, "Information about OCR's Complaint Resolution Procedures," which includes information about OCR's Investigatory Uses of Personal Information.

I am aware that it is the policy of OCR to protect the identity of complainants who cooperate with OCR's investigations. However, I acknowledge that release of my identity to the institution, agency, or other entity named below may be essential to the investigation and enforcement activities conducted by OCR. I give my consent in those limited circumstances when release is required for the processing of the complaint. I also assure OCR that I will cooperate with the complaint resolution activities undertaken on my complaint.

In addition, I acknowledge that under the Freedom of Information Act (FOIA) OCR may be required to disclose information gathered from me pursuant to this investigation. Although no guarantee of confidentiality has been given to me in exchange for information, I have not waived any right to privacy under FOIA that OCR may assert on my behalf.

I understand that the information I provide, as well as other information developed by the investigation, will be used to resolve my complaint against the institution, agency, or other entity named below. I understand that this information will be available to any person within the U.S. Department of Education with a need to know its contents and may be used for program analysis, review, evaluation, and statistical purposes. However, should there be a need to disclose information from the complaint file for reasons other than those already stated, or pursuant to the Privacy Act or the Freedom of Information Act, my prior consent will be solicited.

_____   _____
Date   Signature

                _____
                Please Print or Type Name

_____
Name of the institution, agency, or other
entity against whom your complaint is lodged.

About the Authors

Charles J. Hobson

Charles J. Hobson earned his Ph.D. in Industrial/Organizational Psychology from Purdue in 1981. He is currently an Associate Professor of Business Administration at Indiana University Northwest. Dr. Hobson has 21 years of experience teaching undergraduate and M.B.A. courses in organizational behavior and human resource management. He has served as a consultant and trainer to 130 companies and universities, including several Fortune 500 firms, and functioned as an expert witness in 27 employment discrimination cases, often involving sexual harassment allegations. Dr. Hobson has 103 professional publications/presentations and one book, including an upcoming article in College Student Affairs Journal entitled Sexual Harassment Preventive and Protective Practices at U.S. Colleges and Universities.

In the area of sexual harassment, Dr. Hobson has functioned as a teacher, advisor, consultant, trainer, researcher, and expert witness. He has authored three training handbooks on preventing sexual harassment in higher education from the perspective of students, staff, and faculty. His continuing battles to prevent faculty sexual harassment of students at Indiana University have led to the involvement of Governor Frank O'Bannon, several written complaints with the Department of Education and the EEOC, multiple lawsuits, and testimony against the university.

Colleen L. Hobson

Colleen L. Hobson earned a Bachelor's of Science in Nursing degree from the Medical College of Virginia in 1977, followed by an M.S. in Interdisciplinary Studies from Virginia Commonwealth University in 1984. She has worked in a variety of psychiatric inpatient and outpatient clinical settings with several organizations, including the Psychiatric Institute of Richmond in Richmond, VA; HCA Dominion Hospital in Falls Church, VA; the Visiting Nurses Association in Arlington, VA: Rush Presbyterian-St. Luke's Hospital in Chicago, IL; and the Center for Family Wellness in Schererville, IN. Ms. Hobson is presently employed as a nurse case manager with Genex Corporation in Grand Rapids, MI.

Ms. Hobson has over 12 years of clinical psychiatric experience treating adolescent victims of sexual abuse. She has observed "first hand" the psychological and physical trauma commonly associated with cases involving sexual harassment. A major focus of her work has been on preventing revictimization by enhancing self-esteem, developing self-respecting behavior patterns, and formulating assertive coping strategies to confront potential abusers.